AMERICAN RELATIONS IN THE PACIFIC
AND THE FAR EAST, 1784–1900

PRAEGER SCHOLARLY REPRINTS

Source Books and Studies on the Pacific Area

C. Hartley Grattan, *General Editor*

Hiram Bingham

A RESIDENCE OF TWENTY-ONE YEARS IN THE SANDWICH
ISLANDS; or the Civil, Religious, and Political History of
Those Islands

James Morton Callahan

AMERICAN RELATIONS IN THE PACIFIC AND
THE FAR EAST, 1784–1900

C. F. Gordon Cumming

A LADY'S CRUISE IN A FRENCH MAN-OF-WAR

Walter Coote

THE WESTERN PACIFIC: Being a Description of the Groups of
Islands to the North and East of the Australian Continent

Amasa Delano

A NARRATIVE OF VOYAGES AND TRAVELS IN THE
NORTHERN AND SOUTHERN HEMISPHERES

Dora Hort

TAHITI: The Garden of the Pacific

C. S. Stewart

A VISIT TO THE SOUTH SEAS IN THE U.S. SHIP *VINCENNES*,
DURING THE YEARS 1829 AND 1830; with Scenes in Brazil, Peru,
Manilla, the Cape of Good Hope, and St. Helena

AMERICAN RELATIONS

IN THE

PACIFIC AND THE FAR EAST

1784-1900

By JAMES MORTON CALLAHAN, Ph. D.

PRAEGER PUBLISHERS

New York • Washington • London

PRAEGER PUBLISHERS
111 Fourth Avenue, New York, N.Y. 10003, U.S.A.
5, Cromwell Place, London S.W.7, England

Published in the United States of America in 1969
by Praeger Publishers, Inc.

Introduction © 1969 by Praeger Publishers, Inc.

Library of Congress Catalog Card Number: 69–19859

Printed in the United States of America

INTRODUCTION

The Pacific Ocean has on its shores the seats of several ancient and formidable civilizations. Although this ocean has been part of Europe's global consciousness since the sixteenth century, it has rarely been perceived, and as rarely written about, as an integral whole. Inhabitants of the Pacific Basin—both indigenous peoples and Europeans—have tended to identify themselves with parochial fragments. Through the years, the area has been most commonly divided into the North and South Pacific, with the equator forming a rough dividing line. For those who have accepted this division, the North Pacific has always been the most significant portion, largely because the so-called Far East faces upon it. Because the Pacific region has not been regarded as unitary, much of the writing about Pacific countries and peoples has been partial, fragmentary, or skewed, either in favor of the fraction that is allied to the author's nation, or weighted toward the North Pacific or the Far East. How much this lack of an overview has mattered in the past may be debatable, although I regard it as rather tragic. And I am sure that today there is every reason to try to see the Pacific whole, both historically and contemporaneously. World War II in its Pacific phases involved the entire ocean and most of the countries of its shores; furthermore, the drift of events since the war definitely suggests that, whatever their past orientations, the nations of the Pacific and those on its borders will become increasingly involved with each other.

Over the years, there have been periodic efforts to synthesize in a single work, if not the whole story of the Pacific, at least the record of some nation's activities in it. James

v

Morton Callahan's book is an early effort to present such a comprehensive account of the activities of the Americans in the Pacific Basin. The book seems to have originated as a *pièce d'occasion;* that is, it was based on lectures delivered to graduate students at The Johns Hopkins University, as background for the then recently concluded Spanish-American War. The work offers an accurate turn-of-the-century perspective on the Pacific and, indeed, is important for being just that; how men have seen themselves and their nations *vis à vis* focalizing events or geographical entities is as much the proper concern of the historian as are the events and entities themselves. Callahan's book, then, allows readers to perceive how the Pacific looked to an informed American at the beginning of the twentieth century, at which time Americans had already been active in the Pacific for more than one hundred years. It is notable that, owing to the perspective of his period, Professor Callahan recorded facts and events that were either neglected or forgotten by later writers. However, his own observations were not always accurate or perceptive, indicating that some of his material had not been thoroughly researched; it is also likely that many of the necessary data simply were not to be found in the Baltimore or Washington of Callahan's time. Nevertheless, Dr. Callahan wrote a good and useful book, which remains valuable seven decades after its first publication.

James Morton Callahan was born on a farm in Bedford, Indiana, on November 4, 1864. The Callahans had been settled in the trans-Allegheny West since the end of the American Revolution. James was educated in public schools. In 1883, he completed normal school and began teaching. His early career included service as both a public- and normal-school teacher and as a superintendent of schools. He later enrolled at the University of Indiana, where he received B.A. (1894) and M.A. (1895) degrees. After a summer at the University of Chicago, he went to Johns Hopkins, where, in 1897, he was granted a Ph.D. degree, after having studied history, jurisprudence, politics, and economics. Before receiving this last degree, Callahan had begun teaching at Johns Hopkins and, after an interlude as an acting professor at Hamilton College, he returned to Johns Hopkins as lecturer in diplomatic history. Thus, Callahan appears to have pioneered in an important and widespread academic orientation, "devoting the larger part of his time to the field of American diplomacy and foreign relations (especially to subjects having direct bearing upon present conditions and upon questions of American national policy)." In 1902, he became Professor of History and Political Science at the University of West Virginia; he remained there for the balance of his long life. James Callahan died in 1956 at the age of ninety-two.

C. HARTLEY GRATTAN

AMERICAN RELATIONS

IN THE

PACIFIC AND THE FAR EAST

1784-1900

" The story of America in the Pacific grandly deserves a volume. . . . For over a century we have had an army of pioneers who scarcely dreamed of the magnitude of the movement they were leading."—*Wm. E. Griffis.*

" No one can behold the silent and persevering efforts of our countrymen in the Pacific without a feeling of pride and exultation."—*R. J. Cleveland, 1843.*

" To every lover of his country, as well as to those more immediately concerned in commerce, it must be a pleasing reflection, that a communication is thus happily opened between us and the eastern extremity of the globe."—*Samuel Shaw, 1785.*

" On the whole, it must be a satisfactory consideration to every American, that his country can carry on its commerce with China under advantages, if not in many respects superior, yet in all cases equal, to those possessed by other people."—*Ibid., 1787.*

" The future history of the world must be achieved in the East."—*W. H. Trescot, 1849.*

" Who does not see then, that every year hereafter, European commerce, European politics, European thought and European activity, although actually gaining force, and European connections although actually becoming more intimate, will, nevertheless, sink in importance; while the Pacific ocean, its shores, its islands and the vast region beyond will become the chief theatre of events in the world's great hereafter."—*Senator Seward, 1852.*

" Expansion seems to be recognized, not by the difficulties of resistance, but by the moderation which results from our own internal constitution. . . . Commerce has brought the ancient continents near to us, and created necessities for new positions—perhaps connections or colonies there—and, with the trade and friendship of the elder nations, their conflicts and collisions are brought to our doors and to our hearts. . . . Even prudence will soon be required to decide whether distant regions, either east or west, shall come under our protection, or be left to aggrandize a rapidly spreading and hostile domain of despotism."—*W. H. Seward, 1852.*

SERIES XIX   NOS. 1-3

JOHNS HOPKINS UNIVERSITY STUDIES

IN

HISTORICAL AND POLITICAL SCIENCE

HERBERT B. ADAMS, Editor

History is past Politics and Politics are present History.—*Freeman*

AMERICAN RELATIONS

IN THE

PACIFIC AND THE FAR EAST

1784-1900

BY JAMES MORTON CALLAHAN, PH. D.

BALTIMORE
THE JOHNS HOPKINS PRESS
JANUARY-MARCH, 1901

The Lord Baltimore Press
THE FRIEDENWALD COMPANY
BALTIMORE, MD., U. S. A.

PREFACE

The following chapters on the origin and evolution of American enterprise and policy in the Pacific and the Far East are the outgrowth of a course of lectures delivered by the author in 1899-1900, before graduate students in the department of history and politics of the Johns Hopkins University.

Lectures treating of the relations of the United States with Alaska and Behring Sea, Transandine America, and isthmian transit routes have been reserved for publication elsewhere.

For facilitating my investigations at Washington, D. C., my sincere acknowledgments are due to Mr. Andrew H. Allen, Chief of the Bureau of Rolls and Library of the Department of State, and Messrs. A. P. C. Griffin, Chief Bibliographer, and Hugh A. Morrison, of the Library of Congress. For encouragement in this and other fields of research, I am under obligation to Professor Herbert B. Adams, of Johns Hopkins University.

JAMES MORTON CALLAHAN.

Johns Hopkins University,
Jan. 1, 1901.

CONTENTS

INTRODUCTION.

The Pacific—the sea of Eastern legends—upon whose warm currents unwilling emigrants were carried to primeval America, and a place of interest and excitement which Europe long hoped to reach by some passage across the American continent,[1] for over a century has mirrored upon its waves the silent and persevering efforts of American

[1] The Pacific was unknown to Europeans when Columbus sailed in search of the Indies in 1492, and when England sought a northwest passage in 1497. It was first seen by Balboa from an eminence on the Isthmus of Darien; and after the remarkable voyage of Magellan, in 1520, the " South Sea " became a place of interest and excitement. England, through the influence of her daring buccaneers who appeared on the scene, friends to the sea, but foes to all on its waves, soon rose like a sleeping leviathan to rule the deep. The Cape of Good Hope route to the Indies was found to be better than that by Cape Horn, but the idea of cutting a canal through the Isthmus was early suggested, and the hope of a western passage to the Indies did not finally die out for many years. The English, in the days of Gilbert, had visions of reaching the Pacific by the St. Lawrence, and the early settlers of Jamestown sailed up the Chickahominy with the same thought. Fictitious ideas of wealth to be obtained in the South Pacific resulted in the " South Sea Bubble " and were soon afterwards dispelled by voyages of Wallis, Carteret and later explorers. While the conflict with her American colonies was in progress, England was putting forth efforts to control the commerce of the Northwest coast. In 1776, Captain James Cook was sent to explore the coast and, after discovering the Sandwich Islands, landed at Nootka sound in 1778. He then sailed through Behring Straits, and returned to the Sandwich Islands. All previous voyagers had sailed along the coast of South America to Panama or California, and then across the Pacific to the south of the Sandwich Islands. Cook did not confine himself to former tracks, but made accurate surveys of his own route for the use of subsequent voyagers. Besides the Sandwich Islands he visited the Friendly and Society islands, and New Zealand. He wrote of his discoveries along luxuriant isles and picturesque shores where perfumes were borne on every breeze, and Vancouver and many other explorers followed.

citizens who, trained in the school of hardships, seeking new fields of daring adventure, romance or maritime enterprise, were the pioneers in discovering safe paths and harbors, and in obtaining commercial knowledge of the Pacific, which led the way for American influence in the Far East.

Its waters were navigated by American trading vessels soon after the Revolution. In 1784, the *Empress of China*, fitted out at New York, reached Canton laden with ginseng. Other vessels were soon fitted out in Boston, to engage in trade between China and the Northwest coast—in which Jefferson showed a lively interest. The number of vessels engaged in trade, or in pursuing the sperm whale, soon increased rapidly. Though the danger from French privateers in 1778, the seizures by Spanish authorities at Valparaiso in 1800, the embargo of 1807, the acts of Peruvian corsairs before 1813,[2] and the effects of the War of 1812,[3] were depressing in their effects on enterprise, after 1815 American commerce and fisheries in the Pacific were renewed with vigor and continued to increase.

During the Spanish-American revolution, the influence of American sailors played no unimportant part along the coasts west of the Andes. Even at that early date, a United States consul at Manila, under instructions from Monroe, was studying the conditions in the Philippines, and reporting on the prospects for American trade there. In mid-ocean, the natives were gradually introduced to the virtues of a higher civilization, whose vices, also, they often saw.

As commerce with the islands and the Far East in-

---

[2] In April, 1813, J. R. Poinsett, sent to remonstrate against the acts of the Peruvian corsairs, directed the Chilean army in a successful attack upon the Limian forces.

[3] During the War of 1812 many American whalers in the Pacific were captured and burned or turned into British transports. The island of Nantucket alone lost twenty-seven ships. Captain David Porter, entering the Pacific to protect American interests, destroyed a number of British whalers, and occupied Madison Island as a United States naval and supply station, but was finally defeated by the British near the harbor of Valparaiso.

creased,[4] the necessity of some national protection and supervision[5] induced the American government, after 1825, to keep a naval squadron in the Pacific.[6]   It was the interest of the entire nation to preserve friendly relations with the islands, prevent the evils growing out of desertions and mutinies, investigate the irregular conduct of libertines who were so far removed from the arms of the civil law, and make surveys and charts that would lessen the dangers of shipwreck.[7]   In 1831 the *Potomac* was sent to the coast of distant Sumatra to retaliate upon the natives of Quallah Battoo for their outrageous seizure of an American trading vessel.   For the purpose of protecting and extending commerce with the East, Edmund Roberts, a sea-captain, was sent in 1832 to negotiate treaties and obtain safe ports. After much discussion and delay the United States Exploring Expedition, projected by J. N. Reynolds and others, was organized under Captain Wilkes, and from 1839 to 1841 examined many parts of the Pacific, sailing far toward the south polar regions and northward to the Sandwich Islands and Oregon.

By the settlement of Oregon and the acquisition of California, the United States became almost a neighbor to Russia, Japan and China, and an arbiter in the affairs of the Pacific, the sea of great and increasing activity.   With her keels plowing the waves of the Polynesian world, and the western waters of the Pacific, she soon renewed her efforts to open the gates of the stubbornly exclusive Orient to the commerce of the West, increased her interest in the Sand-

---

[4] By 1829 there were about 100 United States vessels calling at the Hawaiian Islands in a period of 12 months, with a tonnage of 3500 and valued at $5,000,000.

[5] Benjamin Rodman, of New Bedford, writing J. N. Reynolds, June 11, 1836, suggested that a superintending influence over " our marine colonies " was just as important as the establishment of governments and law in our territories.

[6] During the South American revolt the United States had kept a small squadron on the west coast of Chile and Peru.

[7] The log-books of American whalers were a valuable source of information.

wich Islands where conditions after 1850 were preparing the way for a voluntary offer of annexation, took steps to protect American rights to the Guano Islands, contemplated the establishment of distant naval and coaling stations, conducted explorations along the eastern coasts of Asia and in the Northern Pacific, and threatened to bombard the delinquent Fijis.

The Pacific felt the thrill of awakening life, and gradually our back gardens beyond the Cordilleras became front terraces. In 1867 a regular line of steamer service was established between San Francisco and the Asia coast. Soon afterward, Seward, who had watched the growing importance of " the historic sea of the future," purchased Alaska and the Aleutian Islands and brought us within 45 miles of Russia and 700 miles of Japan.

The policy of acquiring distant islands naturally evolved with the course of events. The determination to allow no territorial control which would cut Hawaii adrift from the American system developed into the policy of annexation. The desire to hold a naval station at Pango Pango, led to participation, first, in a tripartite international convention for the neutrality and government of the Samoan Islands, and finally, in an agreement for partition. The logic of history and the exigencies and incidents of the humanitarian war of intervention to end Spanish misrule in Cuba, increasing American opportunity, duty and responsibility, resulted in the acquisition of the Philippines and other islands.

The United States has now become a leading power in international politics, with increased means for the accomplishment of her beneficent mission in the Pacific and the Far East.

CHAPTER I.

PIONEERS IN TRADE AND DISCOVERY.

EARLY COMMERCIAL ENTERPRISES BETWEEN THE AMERICAN COAST AND CHINA.

Maritime enterprise was one of the earliest characteristics of the American people. The colonists soon had many trading vessels. The early settlers, becoming accustomed to work, privations and frugal habits, were led to daring enterprise and determination to secure wealth. The spirit of our fathers on the waves among the fisheries was one cause of the envy that resulted in wars between England and France and America. In 1775 Burke said there was no climate that was not witness to their toil, and no sea but what was vexed by their fisheries " among the tumbling mountains of ice . . . beneath the Arctic circle, into the opposite region of the polar cold, on the coast of Africa, and along the coasts of Brazil." In the school of hardships, the Americans had even become able to capture the vessels of the British during the Revolution. American privateers, by prolonging the conflict on the waves, made success possible.

No sooner had the war closed than American merchants, seeking to be among the first to engage in direct trade with the Far East, fitted out vessels to sail the Pacific.[1] The American flag first appeared at Canton, China, during the " Canton War," in 1784, upon the *Empress of China*, which,

---

[1] There had been an early American trade with China, via British vessels, tea being received in return for ginseng, which was purchased from New England Indians who received their pay in money, calico and trinkets.

having been fitted out for the China trade by Daniel Parker & Co., sailed from New York via Strait of Sunda, in February of that year, laden with ginseng.[2] Samuel Shaw, the supercargo of the *Empress*, was appointed consul to Canton in 1786. At that time, John Ledyard, of Connecticut, who had accompanied Captain Cook around the world, and now desired to engage in trade with the Northwest coast and Canton,[3] was at Paris talking with Jefferson, at whose suggestion he undertook to go, via Russia, Siberia and Kamschatka, to explore the western part of America.[4]

---

[2] Diplomatic Correspondence of the U. S., 1783-89, vol. vii. Samuel Shaw to John Jay, May 19, 1785.

Major Shaw wrote a full account of his relations with China and Batavia. [Josiah Quincy: Journals of Major Samuel Shaw ... with a life of the author. Boston, 1847. 360 pp.] Soon after reaching China on his first voyage, he had occasion to cooperate with the British, who had so recently been our enemies in war. A British gunner, while firing a salute, killed a Chinaman. The Chinese officials asked the delivery of the gunner, and, failing in their demand, they finally seized Mr. Smith, the supercargo of the British vessel. The Europeans unanimously agreed to make common cause, and the Americans joined. Shaw, at the request of the British, ordered his vessel to Canton to help enforce the demand for the release of the supercargo, and was the last to leave. The British submitted, however, and agreed to deliver the gunner. The harmony maintained between the Americans and the British was particularly noticeable by the French, who had been our recent allies. After his return to New York in May, 1785, Shaw wrote John Jay, the United States Minister for Foreign Affairs, an account of his voyage. He soon received a reply which stated that Congress felt "a peculiar satisfaction in the successful issue of the first effort of the citizens of America to establish direct trade with China." After he returned to Canton, in January, 1787, as the first American consul to China, he wrote Jay a long letter in which he said: "On the whole, it must be a satisfactory consideration to every American, that his country can carry on its commerce with China under advantages, if not in many respects superior, yet in all cases equal, to those possessed by other people."

[3] Jared Sparks: Life of John Ledyard. Jefferson's Works, vol. i, p. 68.

[4] On returning to America in 1782, he had induced Robert Morris to take an active interest in the northwest trade, and to begin to fit out a vessel, but Morris finally abandoned the enterprise on account of pecuniary embarrassments.

Failing to receive the permission of the Empress of Russia, but still hoping to be " the first circumambulator of the earth," with " only two shirts and yet more shirts than shillings," he continued his journey eastward over Siberia until he was arrested when within 200 miles of Kamschatka. Jefferson already saw the commercial and political significance of the region, and had received impressions which later led to the expedition of Lewis and Clarke, who were sent to determine whether the Missouri and Columbia rivers would afford a practicable route to the Pacific.

In 1787, the *Canton* (Capt. Thos. Truxton), the old *Alliance* (Capt. John Reed), and no less than three other vessels were engaged in the China trade. In the same year, shrewd New England merchants, seeking new fields of commerce between the Northwest coast and Canton, also sent the *Columbia* (Captain Kendrick) and the sloop *Lady Washington* (Captain Gray) to the vacant lands south of the Straits of Fuca to trade, explore, buy lands of the natives and build stores and forts. The captains were provided with sea letters issued by the United States Government, passports by Massachusetts, and letters of recommendation from the Spanish plenipotentiary in the United States. The vessels became separated in a storm, after rounding Cape Horn (January, 1788). The *Washington* reached Nootka sound on September 17, 1788, a few days before the *Columbia*, and spent the winter there. In the following summer she sailed northward, and Gray saw islands which he named Washington Islands in honor of George Washington. They had already been called Prince Edward's Islands by the British, and are now known as the Charlotte group. Captain Kendrick afterward took command of the *Washington* to sail with Captain William Douglas, of the *Grace.*[5]

The *Columbia,* by her appearance in the Pacific, " agitated

---

[5] Joseph Ingraham: Journal of the Voyage of the Brigantine *Hope,* from Boston to the Northwest coast of America. 4 vols., in MS. at Dept. of State.

half of the Spanish dominion in America." [6]   In May, 1788, she entered the harbor of the island of Juan Fernandez for repairs. Ambrose O'Higgins, the Captain-General of Chile, arrested and cashiered the Spanish commandant who gave the vessel friendly treatment. Lacroix, the viceroy of Peru, sent a ship from Callao in pursuit, and requested the authorities on the coasts of Chile, Peru and Mexico, to seize any foreign vessel which should appear. Notwithstanding the alertness of the Spanish officials toward the south, the American vessels were not disturbed by the Spanish authorities at Nootka.

The *Columbia*, after remaining at Nootka until October, 1789, carried furs to Canton, exchanged them for teas, completed the circumnavigation of the earth,[7] and in August, 1790, her return was celebrated at Boston with much enthusiasm.[8]   Captain Ingraham, the mate, brought with him from the Sandwich Islands a native crown prince, Opye, who became the centre of interest, and whose visit was the beginning of our friendship with Hawaii.

Other American vessels had recently stopped at the Sandwich Islands, and had not been favorably impressed with the character of the natives.[9]   In the latter part of 1789 the *Eleanor*, an American armed trading vessel, commanded by Captain Metcalf, of New York, stopped *en*

---

[6] Since the royal ordinance of 1692, every foreign vessel in those seas, without a license from Spain, had been treated as an enemy. The fur traders in the North Pacific excited the apprehensions of the Spanish Government.

[7] The *Columbia* was the first vessel to carry our flag around the world. In 1789 there were fifteen American vessels at Canton. The number largely increased in a decade. According to the Canton custom-house record, 20 ships and two brigs from the United States visited that port from June 11, 1800, to April 27, 1801. For the year ending June, 1802, there were 29 ships and 2 brigs. From June, 1802, to January 9, 1803, there were 31 ships and 1 schooner. [Pitkin: Statistical View, N. Y., 1817. p. 246, and Appendix No. 2.]

[8] The *Massachusetts*, built for China trade, had sailed for Canton on March 28, 1790. See Delano's " Voyages."

[9] John White: Voyage to the South Sea, Boston, 1823.

route to China.   Natives stole a small boat in order to get
nails and iron, and Metcalf, a few days later, took revenge
by firing into a crowd, who had come in canoes
to trade, and killed many innocent persons.[10].   The *Fair
American*, commanded by Metcalf, after having been detained at Nootka, arrived a few days later, and was captured
by natives, who proceeded to kill all on board except
Isaac Davis.   The latter's life was saved by interposition
of one Ridler, the carpenter's mate of the *Columbia*, who
had remained at Hawaii.   Davis and John Young, an Englishman, were detained, and finally became chiefs, and instructed natives in the use of firearms.   The natives were
preparing 26,000 canoes to attack Captain Metcalf's brig,
a few miles away, while pretending to be trading, but the
Americans on the island exaggerated the power of Metcalf's
guns and obtained permission of the king to send a letter
requesting the captain to depart, but not stating what had
occurred.   Six months later, Captain Douglas, in the
schooner *Grace*, arrived, and sent a letter requesting the delivery of the whites that remained, but failed to get them.
He left Young and James Cox in care of the king to over-
see the collection of sandalwood for the China market.[11]

From a financial standpoint the voyage of the *Columbia*
was not a success, but the enterprising Bostonians were determined not to neglect the " infant and lucrative China
trade."   Among the first, after the return of the *Columbia*,
to reembark for the Pacific was Captain Joseph Ingraham.

---

[10] Ingraham's Journal, vol. ii, p. 70.   Greenhow: History of
Oregon and California (Boston, 1845), chap. x, p. 224.

[11] The sandalwood traffic soon became important, and was a
valuable source of revenue for the Hawaiian chiefs.   Kamehameha
compelled the natives to go on long journeys to the interior in
search for sandalwood trees, and to hew the wood and bring it to
the coast where he exchanged it for guns and vessels, by means of
which, he made himself master of his own and then the surrounding islands.   The wood was carried to China by the traders who
exchanged it for teas and silk.   The supply in a few years became
much decreased.

2

At the Department of State [12] are four interesting volumes of an illustrated manuscript journal in which he has given an account of his voyage and descriptions of the natives wherever he found them. On September 16, 1790, taking Opye with him, he accepted the command of the brigantine *Hope*, bade an affecting farewell to his native shores,[13] and again braved the perilous ocean, sailing via Cape Horn.

In April, 1791, he reached the Marquesas Islands, discovered by Spain in 1595, and anchored a mile and a half off the shore, where naked savages, men and women, came swimming and in canoes, bringing a pig and cocoanuts. Opye went on shore to buy water, of which the natives soon brought a plentiful supply, likewise of wood, bananas, small pigs, etc., which they exchanged for small nails. They had little knowledge of iron, and showed much curiosity. They became so bold in climbing the sides of the vessel that it was found necessary to drive them away. They had, also, a propensity for stealing, but immediately returned articles when they were discovered. The females diverted the attention of the sentinels from the frying pans and cooking utensils, which they proceeded to appropriate. At night they drew off and gave the crew a partial rest from their intolerable noise; but at daylight they came again, " swimming like a torrent," and bringing more wood and water. About 60 canoes with 600 persons, some with horse-palm umbrellas, collected around the vessel. The male natives, not being allowed to come on board, for fear they would divert the crew from their work, became very troublesome. The young men, notwithstanding the efforts of the older ones to check them, swam under the bottom of the vessel, and, with long poles, broke the cabin windows, and one of them struck Ingraham with a stick of wood. They all

---

[12] They probably came into the possession of the United States Government shortly before the settlement of the Oregon question.

[13] The *Hope* was soon followed by the *Columbia*, then the *Hancock*, the *Jefferson*—and also by the *Margaret*, of New York.

seemed sorry, however, when the boat was preparing to leave.

No observations were made on shore. Opye, the only one who landed, said the women crowded about him so thickly that in his efforts to pay attention to them he could see nothing else. The fact that many men were seen with only one eye indicated that peace did not reign supreme.

On April 19, 1791, Ingraham, near latitude 8° 7′ South and longitude 140° West, unexpectedly found several islands not indicated on the charts of the Spaniards or of Cook. He named them Washington, Adams, Federal, Lincoln, Franklin, Hancock and Knox.[14] He intended to go on shore, but finding no convenient place to anchor, he called together his men, and was greeted with cheers when he announced that the islands were newly discovered and belonged to the United States.[15]

On May 20, Ingraham reached "Owhyhee" [Hawaii], where a hundred trading canoes soon brought plenty of hogs, pigs, fowls and potatoes. Proceeding to Mowee, where 200 canoes soon collected, he received on board Tianna and "Tommahammahan," who were at war with Titierce and Tio. Feeling that the natives desired an opportunity to make an attack, he refused to go nearer shore as requested by Tianna, who said it took the natives' breath to bring hogs so far. Leaving Opye, he went farther along the coast, and found three white men, recently left by an American vessel, who warned him that the natives would take the first opportunity to capture his vessel. After finding it necessary to fire upon some of the natives, he saw about "700 canoes and 20,000 fighting men" collecting around him, and taking the whites with him he retired. Pyamano, a son of Chief Titierce, remained on board, intending to go to America; but Ingraham, not desiring to

---

[14] Captain Roberts, of Boston, in 1792, named some of them Adams, Jefferson, Hamilton and Madison.

[15] When Ingraham reached Macao he learned that the French had discovered four of the islands twenty days later.

carry away a great chief, nor wanting to give the natives more chance to lament that they had ever been discovered by civilization, and, probably influenced by the arrival of a canoe from the windward to announce a declaration of war, discharged him at the next trading place.

On June 1, the *Hope* sailed from the Sandwich Islands, and on June 29 reached Washington Islands on the North-west coast (Prince Edward's or Charlotte's isles) where repairs were made, and water and wood obtained. On July 4, the crew killed a hog, dined on the shore, and drank to the President's health. Sailing farther to the north to "Port Ingraham," they were approached by women natives, who came in canoes singing and offering to sell their foul fish. Chief Cow agreed to have skins brought, and soon other tribes sought to trade in fur. After reaching 54° 21′ N. and starting to return southward, the *Hope* met the *Columbia* July 23, on its second voyage.[16] Going on board, Ingraham received letters from Boston, and learned from Captain Gray that the Spaniards had augmented their settlement at Nootka and established another in the Straits of Juan de Fuca. He was not willing to concede that Spain could claim the entire Northwest coast by right of discovery. Contemplating the recent disturbance between Spain and England, and the possibility of three other nations contending for the territory claimed by each of these powers, he was about to lay out the whole Northwest coast and assign to each his lot, but decided to leave the question for national assemblies to discuss when it should become a matter of more serious consequence.

After more trading with the natives toward the south of the Washington Islands (some of whom offered to go to "fight for more skins"), the *Hope*, on September 2, sailed away, and, on October 6, reached "Owhyhee," where Ingraham

---

[16] In June, 1791, the Columbia started on a second voyage under the command of Captain Gray, who discovered the mouth of the Columbia river, giving to the United States an advantage in the trade between China and the Northwest coast.

found the brig *Hancock,* of Boston, bound for Macaσ. While the natives were trading, the king's son again came on board with the desire to go to America. Starting on October 12, the *Hope* reached China on November 27. At Macao roads, Ingraham was informed by Captain R. D. Coolidge (who had formerly been on the *Washington,* but had become commander of the *Grace* after the death of Douglas) that China, on account of being at war with Russia, prohibited fur ships from entering the port of Canton, but he disposed of part of his furs there and left the others to be sold by Captain John Canning, of the *Nonsuch.* Two other American vessels arrived from the Northwest coast in the early part of December. One was the brig *Washington* (Captain John Kendrick), which had been in Nootka sound while Spain still held possession. The other was the *Snow Fairy* (Captain William Rogers), recently the property of Douglas.

Ingraham left Canton June 22, 1792, and in April sailed from Macao to Nootka, where, on July 2, he and Gray sent a joint letter to the Spanish commander. In November, after a twenty-two days' sail, he reached " Owhyhee," where his " Journal " suddenly ends.

The direct trade of the North Pacific between the American coasts and China soon grew in its importance, and remained almost entirely in the hands of Americans until 1814. After 1784, when the Northwest Company was organized at Montreal, the latter took the place of New York as the principal seat of the lake fur trade; but the Northwest and Hudson Bay companies became involved in disputes with each other, which resulted to the advantage of the Americans in the Pacific trade, which for twenty-five years was carried almost exclusively by vessels from Boston. It finally declined on account of the scarcity and high price of furs, caused by the competition of the Russians who advanced southward."[17] The American vessels usually

---

[17] R. J. Cleveland: Narrative of Voyages and Commercial Enterprises, 1792-1818. 2 vols. Cambridge, 1843.

started with valuable cargoes of West India productions and British manufactured articles—many with knives, iron, copper pans, and various trinkets for the natives—perhaps gathered a few seal skins or butts of oil in the South Pacific or obtained turtle at the Galapagos, sold a few articles at Valparaiso, bartered with the natives of the Northwest coast for furs, completed their cargo with sandalwood and other articles at the Sandwich Islands, and exchanged everything for teas, silks and nankins at Canton. On these voyages the Americans used the Sandwich Islands as a principal place of resort, but they also visited islands in all parts of the Pacific.[18] Their industry finally resulted in the settlement of Astoria and the colonization of Oregon, and contributed to the establishment of American influence along the western coast of South America, in the islands of the Pacific, and in the Far East.

The early occupation and enterprise of Americans in the Pacific was not limited to the trade between the Northwest coast, Hawaii and China. Many were engaged in whaling and sealing, and some in obtaining the pearl oyster and bêche-de-mer. In 1791 six ships from Nantucket, and one from New Bedford, sailed for the Pacific to pursue the sperm whale, which had fled from his old haunts in the Atlantic.[19] Notwithstanding the dangers and hardships incident to the occupation, the number of vessels engaged in

---

[18] They also furnished the Russian-American settlements with European articles in exchange for furs. In 1809 Russia complained of the "illicit" trade of American citizens on the North Pacific coasts. Later, Count Romanzoff, the Russian Minister of Foreign Affairs, at St. Petersburg, proposed to J. Q. Adams, the American plenipotentiary, an arrangement allowing Americans to supply the Russian settlements on the Pacific with provisions and manufactures, and transport the furs of the Russian Company to Canton, under the condition that they abstain from all intercourse with the natives of the Northwest coast. To this Mr. Adams explained that he could not agree. [Greenhow: History of Oregon and California, chapter xiv.]

[19] Alexander Starbuck: History of the American Whale Fishery.

it rapidly increased and exceeded that of any other nation.[20] The thrilling excitement of chasing such gigantic game had a tinge of the romantic, and made privations more easily endured. " The blood more stirs to rouse a lion than to start a hare." Sometimes there were exciting races be- tween English and American vessels for the same whale, and when the agility of the American sailor won by success- fully throwing his ponderous harpoon, he was greeted with repeated shouts of applause.[21]

The plan of getting seals in the South Seas for the China trade was early undertaken. Mr. Edmund Fanning tells us in his " Voyages Around the World," that in May, 1792, the brig *Betsey*, under Captain Steele, and owned by Mr. Nexsen, left New York upon such an expedition by way of Cape Verde and Falkland islands, but it never reached Canton. In 1797, Fanning, as commander of the *Betsey*, sailed by the same route to the Pacific, and after visiting Washington, Fanning and other islands, reached Macao and Canton. He found living on Tinian Island Mr. Swain, of Nantucket, and several others who had escaped from a wrecked English vessel. Among them were the widow and servant woman of the captain. On the route back to New York he defeated a band of pirates.

In January, 1800, the *Aspasia*, with twenty-two guns, was sent by New York gentlemen to explore and get seals in the South Seas. She was commissioned by the United States Government as a letter of marque. At Valparaiso she was detained by Spanish officials, who suspected that she was a British ship-of-war.[22] She continued her voyage to Canton and returned to New York, but part of her cargo

---

[20] In June, 1795, and again in May, 1811, the British Parliament passed an act offering premiums in order to encourage British fisheries in the South Seas. The act also encouraged Americans to reside in England except when on the whaling voyage. The United States offered no bounty.

[21] See an article in the N. Am. Rev., Jan., 1834.

[22] Fanning's Voyages around the World, etc., 1792-1832. Boston, 1833.

was lost by a wreck and the adventure resulted in no financial gain. The brig *Union,* under Captain Pendleton, left
New York on a similar voyage by way of Sydney, and to
the Fiji Islands, and in 1803, Delano, who had sailed to
China in the *Perseverance* by way of Hawaii in 1799, went
directly across from Peru to Canton,[23] stopping at Lobos
Islands and Wake Island.

A few Americans reached the Fiji Islands early in the
century. Charles Savage, reputed to be an honest sailor
belonging to the American brig *Eliza,* which was wrecked
in the Fijis in 1808, became a kind of " head man " at Bau,
the Fijian capital. His influence in the government probably was due to the disturbed condition of the islands and
the presence of several shipwrecked and runaway seamen,
and of twenty-six convicts who had escaped from New
South Wales in 1804.[24] Firmly established at Bau, he demanded and received some of the " highest ladies of the
realm " for wives,[25] but his children were all still-born, and
his hopes to establish white sway were wrecked. The
arrivals from New South Wales died out rapidly by fights
or irregular life in the hot climate.[26] Savage was put to
death and eaten in March, 1814.

By the close of Jefferson's administration American interests in the Pacific were of sufficient importance to attract
the attention of the Government. In the spring of 1812
President Madison gave Fanning a commission as commander of an expedition of discovery, to consist of the ships
Volunteer and *Hope,* and to go to the southern hemisphere
and voyage around the world. Secretary Monroe furnished
him letters from European ambassadors and consuls rec-
ommending him to the kindness and protection of vessels
and officials of their nationality. When the expedition was
nearly ready, war with England was declared which prevented it from sailing.

---

[23] Delano's Voyages. Boston, 1818.   [24] Seemann, p. 406.
[25] Capt. I. Erksine: Western Pacific, p. 197.
[26] Dillon: Discovery of the Fate of de la Pérouse.

CHAPTER II.

OCCUPATION OF MADISON ISLAND IN THE WAR OF 1812.

One of the most interesting American episodes in the Pacific is the formal occupation of Madison Island by Captain David Porter in 1813, while he was engaged in protecting American whaling interests in that vicinity.

Before the declaration of war with England in 1812, American whalemen on the coast of Peru often suffered from the piratical acts of Peruvian privateers, who also cut them out from Chile ports where they had gone to recruit.[1] J. R. Poinsett, of South Carolina, was sent to remonstrate, but when the Anglo-American war began, he found that the corsairs, as a fresh pretext for plunder, claimed they were allies of England.[2] Learning that an expedition sent by the authorities of Lima had captured Concepcion and Talcahuano, and that at the latter place a Limian armament of two men-of-war and 1500 troops was detaining many American vessels, he resolved to resort to stronger measures than those of diplomacy. Joining the Chilean army, he directed its movements until the enemy was driven from the town and the whalemen released. Though Lima yielded to muskets and cannon, her depredations did not entirely cease until the arrival of Captain Porter in the United States frigate *Essex*, the first United States ship-of-war to spread her sails in the Pacific.

On October 6, 1812, Porter had received his orders for

---

[1] Alex. Starbuck: History of the American Whale Fishery.
[2] Porter: Journal of a Cruise in the Pacific, 1812-14. N. Y., 1822.

a long cruise. After reaching the South Atlantic, he had learned that the people in Buenos Ayres were starving, and unable to supply his wants, and that Montevideo was invincible. He at once shaped his course for the Pacific, and on March 15 landed at Valparaiso, where he was astonished to learn that Chile had declared her independence from Spain, and that the viceroy of Peru had sent out cruisers against American shipping.[3]

Porter's appearance in the Pacific was of great importance to American whaling interests. He at once proceeded to destroy unfriendly vessels, and to break up the British whale fisheries off the coast of Chile and Peru. After capturing British property worth two and a half million dollars, and 360 British seamen, whom he liberated on parole, he decided to seek a place of safety where he could put his ship in a condition to return home, and, at the same time, give his men some amusement.

Sailing to the group discovered by Ingraham in 1791, he anchored at Madison Island (Nukuhiva, or Sir Henry Martin's Island), which he proceeded to occupy for the United States, and to conquer and make them tributary to the United States by the request and assistance of the friendly tribes. He built Fort Madison (4 guns) and a village which he called Madisonville. The waters where he anchored, he named Massachusetts bay. In taking formal occupation on November 19, 1813, Porter declared that the natives by their own request, and in order to render secure the United States claim to the island, were adopted into the great American family; and that they, on their part, had promised to give welcome hospitality and protection to American citizens who visited the islands, and also to endeavor to prevent subjects of Great Britain from coming among them during the continuation of the War of 1812.

In his declaration, which he read, he said: " Our rights

---

[3] Navy Dept. Tracts, vol. xiv, No. 22; Essex Inst. Hist. Coll., vol. x. Salem, 1870.

to this island being founded on priority of discovery, conquest and possession, cannot be disputed . . . Influenced by considerations of humanity, which promise speedy civilization . . . as well as by views of policy, which secure to my country a fruitful and populous island, possessing every advantage of security and supplies for vessels, and which, of all others, is the most happily situated, as respects climate and local position, I do declare that I have in the most solemn manner, under the American flag displayed at Fort Madison, and in the presence of numerous witnesses, taken possession of said island, called Madison Island, for the use of the United States . . . ; and that the act of taking possession was announced by seventeen guns. . . . And that our claim to this island may not hereafter be disputed, I have buried in a bottle, at the foot of the flagstaff in Fort Madison, a copy of this instrument, together with several pieces of money, the coin of the United States."[4]   This deed was signed by Porter, nine United States naval officers and others.

While on the island the American forces intervened to secure peace between the natives, and joined the friendly tribes in their wars against the Happahs.

On December 13, Porter sailed for Valparaiso, leaving Lieut. Gamble in command with four prize ships, twenty-one marines and six prisoners. He reported that he had completely broken up British navigation on the Pacific, and injured her navigation to the extent of two and one-half million dollars. In the following March, however, after a desperate encounter[5] outside the port, watched by thousands of witnesses from surrounding hills, he was compelled to surrender to Commodore Hillyar, of the British navy, who had recently arrived with the *Phoebe* and the

---

[4] Capt. D. Porter: Journal of a Cruise to the Pacific in 1812-14. N. Y., 1822.

[5] Poinsett, during the engagement, requested the Governor of Valparaiso to protect the *Essex*, but his request was not granted. He left the country soon after.

Cherub. He and part of his crew, on parole, were allowed to sail for New York on the *Essex, Junior.* Several of the crew of the *Essex,* who were left at Valparaiso, enlisted in the " patriot " army at Santiago.

Gamble found his stay at Madison Island far from pleasant. His life was rendered miserable by rains and squalls, and by the character of his crew, some of whom were worthless and ready to desert at every opportunity. He was also much troubled by the natives, who showed signs of attack and soon began to kill the swine left by Porter. Threats of devastation being insufficient to prevent theft by some of the natives, he found it necessary to attack and chasten them. After they had fled and the chiefs offered to replace the swine, he asked an indemnity for his trouble and also demanded the surrender of the thieves, whom the chiefs claimed they could not apprehend, but finally closed the affair by exacting a promise of future vigilance. Later, when intertribal quarrels and wars were renewed, he successfully restored tranquillity by intervention. Supplies becoming precarious, he sailed to other islands to barter iron for swine and vegetables, and at almost every place he landed the natives asked his aid in intertribal wars which had arisen chiefly over fishery regulations or property. But he had enough to engage his attention in watching and punishing his own men, who went to sleep on watch, or permitted the clandestine visits of female natives, or left camp without permission or under pretence of washing their clothes at a distant brook. Early in May, seven men on deck defiantly refused to work, bound and imprisoned Gamble and others, hoisted the English flag, spiked the guns at the fort, took the powder and other materials and set sail. Gamble again had reason to become alarmed at the natives, who began to repeat their thefts and finally attacked the ships, massacring four midshipmen.

Burning one of his vessels, with seven men and a leaky ship without a boat or anchor, he sailed to Owyhee (Hawaii) for supplies and men. In June, after he had started to return to Valparaiso, he was captured by the British warship *Cherub*. Reaching Valparaiso (on September 23), where he was entertained by the American vice-consul, Blanco, he heard the strange news that Wellington had been sent to the United States with 20,000 troops and created Emperor of North America! He finally arrived at New York in August, 1815.

Though Madison Island was afterwards recommended as a convenient location for a naval and supply station, the United States never took any step toward occupation.

Porter published an account of his experience in the Pacific, in which he described the natives and made numerous references to the beauty and grace of the native women, who roamed at pleasure and were promiscuous in their intercourse with the sailors. The English *Quarterly Review* ridiculed him for occupying the island, and severely criticised him for his voluptuous descriptions of the island beauties, and for the freedom which he permitted between them and the sailors, as well as for cruelty to the natives. Porter, in reply, after stating that Ingraham's discovery of 1791 gave the United States a just claim to the island, referred to the license of the sailors under Captain Cook and others, and to previous writers, who had described feasts with native women. In defending himself from the charge of cruelty, he presented the British record in the Pacific on that score, and stated that men away from law and in danger, must judge of the means of safety and act according to circumstances. He declared that the safety of his ships, prizes and men depended upon maintaining a position on the island, and that it was necessary to conciliate the natives by joining them against their enemies.

CHAPTER III.

EARLY AMERICAN INTERESTS ON THE PACIFIC COAST.

American interests on the Pacific coast increased with the number of American ships sailing between that region and China, though its political importance for the United States attracted little attention until 1803, when President Jefferson sent Meriwether Lewis and William Clarke to explore along the Missouri and trace some convenient stream to the Pacific with a view of opening an inland trade route.[1] Jefferson favored every reasonable facility and patronage by the Government to encourage the trade of United States citizens with that distant region.[2] In 1810 he considered that an early settlement on the western coast would be a " great public acquisition," and looked forward to the time " when its descendants should spread themselves throughout the whole length of the coast," covering it with free Americans, independent and self-governing. By invitation, and the offer of government protection, he encouraged Astor to fit out a vessel with seed and provisions and to send 120 persons (some by sea and others by the overland route) to the mouth of the Columbia, where in 1811 they established the American settlement of Astoria.[3]

Astor had long been engaged in commerce and trade between the Northwest coast and China. For the purpose of securing such a control of that trade as to lessen the danger of rivalry by the Northwest Company, in 1810, at

---

[1] Lewis and Clarke: Expedition, etc. Phila., 1814.
[2] Jefferson's Works, vol. vi. To John Jacob Astor, May 24, 1812.
[3] Washington Irving: Astoria.

New York, he assisted in the organization of the Pacific Fur Company with himself at its head. For clerks and *voyageurs* he selected principally Canadians. Macdougal, who was appointed to superintend the new enterprise, sailed in the *Tonquin* in September, 1810. At Owyhee, in February, 1811, he made an unsuccessful attempt to negotiate a treaty with Kamehameha, but he obtained supplies, and also men, to engage in service on the coast. His settlement at Astoria, near the mouth of the Columbia, was joined in January, 1812, by the overland detachment of sixty men, who had endured many hardships and dangers on the route. On May 5, 1812, the *Beaver* arrived with more men from the United States and with 36 Sandwich islanders. In January, 1813, the community, already embarrassed by the destruction of the *Tonquin* and her crew by the Indians near the entrance to the Straits of Fuca, was thrown into gloom by the news that the United States had declared war against Great Britain. On October 16 the Canadian managers of the company entered into an agreement by which all the establishments, furs and stock were sold to the Northwest Company for $58,000. The captain of a British vessel, which arrived soon after, hauled down the American flag, replaced it by the British flag, and changed the name of the place to Fort George. Astor, on hearing the news, considered the sale disgraceful.[4]

In 1815 Monroe demanded the restitution of the post. Two years later he sent the *Ontario* to establish a settlement on the Columbia. When Castlereagh expressed regret and a desire to avoid collision, Secretary Adams wrote Rush, at London, that it had not been anticipated that England would be disposed to start questions of title with us on the shores of the South Sea, stating that she would hardly find it useful or wise to resist every possibility of extension to our national dominion.

The expansive designs of Russia in America were a

---

[4] Greenhow: History of Oregon and California, chap. xiv.

source of some concern to officials of the United States Government. Prevost, the United States agent who had received the surrender of Astoria by the British, in a letter to Adams dated at Monterey, November 11, 1818, after referring to the Russian settlements made in 1816 at the Sandwich Islands and near the harbor of San Francisco, said: "May we not infer views to the early possession of this harbor, ultimately to the sovereignty of entire California. Surely the growth of a race, scarcely emerged from the savage state, on these shores is to be deprecated, and should excite the jealousies of the United States and induce her to preserve a station, which may serve as a barrier to northern aggrandizement."

Floyd's Report [5] in the House in January, 1821, estimating that there were already $8,000,000 of property owned by the United States in the Pacific, and calling attention to Russia's menaces against Turkey, Persia, Japan, China and Spanish America, and her plans to command the North Pacific, urged the propriety of taking energetic steps to guard our increasing interests on the Columbia, whose valley, Benton thought, might soon become the granary of China and Japan, who had not yet opened diplomatic relations with us. It was suggested that settlement of the country might be facilitated by the immigration of Chinese. Though the friends of the report, in support of their views, emphasized the importance of fisheries and trade with China, and spoke of possible growth of the lumber trade, and of agriculture, in the future, the members of the House gave the subject little discussion and voted to table it. The majority probably considered such an extension of the Union chimerical. Tucker (of the opposition) of Virginia, said necessarily the Rockies always would be an impassable barrier between interests.

Russia had not only made establishments in California and Hawaii, but threatened to enforce the Russian claim

---

[5] Rp. Com. 45, 16-2, Jan. 25, 1821.

to make the Pacific a *mare clausum* north of 51° on the American coast and 45° on the Asiatic coast. An edict of Alexander, September 4, 1821, under pretext of preventing smuggling, stated rules for limits of the navigation and communication along the coast of East Siberia, the Northwest coast of America to 51°, the Aleutian, Kurile and other islands, and prohibiting foreign vessels from coming nearer than 100 Italian miles to these places, except in gales or when in need of provisions, etc. President Monroe was surprised at the Russian claim to 51°, etc., and Secretary Adams, February 25, 1822, asked Poletica, the Russian minister, to explain the Russian grounds of right.

Poletica, in a long reply, of February 28, denying that Spain had ever had a right to claim north of 42°, said 51° was only a mean point between the Russian establishment of New Archangel at 57° and the American colony on the Columbia at 46°. In justification of the 100-mile prohibition, he said that the foreign adventurers, nearly all of whom were American citizens, by their illicit trade and irregular conduct, and by selling arms to natives of Russian America, had been the source of pressing but unsuccessful remonstrances from the time when Russia began diplomatic correspondence with the United States, and that coercion, though not conceived in a hostile spirit, or to strike a blow at maritime interests of the United States, had become a necessity.[6]

Adams could not understand how Russia could claim to 51° when she had only claimed to 55° in 1799, and was persuaded that American citizens would remain unmolested as heretofore in exercising their right to sell to the natives of Northwest America. He had no proof that the trade had been exercised in a spirit unfriendly to Russia. In his reply of March 30, he said that the right of the United States to navigate the seas near Behring, as well as elsewhere, was a part of our independence, and that her ves-

---

[6] Exec. Papers, 112, 7-1, vol. vi, Apr. 15, 1822.

sels had exercised that right from the period of her existence as a nation.   In reply to Poletica's suggestion that
Russia had a right to exclude foreigners from the sea
north of 51° in America and 45° in Asia, Adams reminded
him that the distance between those two points was only
about 4000 miles.

Poletica, in a letter of (March 21) April 2, referred to eight
Russian settlements in latitude 48° and 49° (462 persons)
existing as late as 1789, and ventured to say that the great
width of the Pacific would not prevent Russia from making
it a closed sea, but he referred the matter to his government.

After the protests of the United States and Great Britain,
Russia suspended her edict, and soon after Monroe's fam-
ous message of 1823, she granted the right of United States
citizens to fish along the coasts of Russian America, except in the rivers and harbors; but, after 10 years, believing
that the privilege had been abused, she refused to renew
the agreement for allowing either fishing or trading.[7]   Thus
was the way prepared for the future acquisition of Alaska
and the islands skirting the Behring sea.

The Americans, at an early day, also exercised considerable influence along the Pacific coast of Spanish America.
R. J. Cleveland, in his "Voyages," tells us that as early as
1802 our sailors were advocating self-government to the
people of Chile at Valparaiso.   The revolution which
opened in Chile, in 1817, gave a stimulus to American
trade[8] and induced the United States to keep a small squadron on the west coast of Peru and Chile.   With the eman-
cipation of all Spanish America from the colonial rule of
the mother country, Americans stopped more frequently
along the west coast of Mexico and California.

The growth of American commerce and whaling interests

---

[7] Van Buren's Message of Dec., 1838.

[8] For an account of affairs on the coast of South America, 1817-20,
see "Voyages" of R. J. Cleveland, who undertook a voyage under
the auspices of John Jacob Astor.

in the Pacific and the Far East, during the administration
of Monroe and J. Q. Adams, and the desire for ports essential to their protection, induced the Jackson administration,
in 1835, to seek for the acquisition of territory north of
37° that would include the bay of San Francisco, and to
undertake negotiations for purchase, but in vain.   In December, 1841, Upshur, Secretary of State under Tyler,
knowing that Americans were settling in California, and
considering that the increasing commerce of the United
States within the Gulf of California, and to San Francisco,
together with the weakness of the local authorities, rendered
it " proper that occasional countenance and protection
should be afforded to American enterprise in that quarter,"
instructed Commander Thomas ap Catesby Jones to . . .
" examine bays and harbors in the interest of commerce and
science."

In May, on reaching Callao bay, Jones learned that a
strong French squadron had sailed from Valparaiso in
March, 1842.   He strongly suspected that its purpose was
to colonize or occupy California, or the Sandwich Islands,
or the Washington Islands[9] [a part of the Marquesas group].
His anxiety was increased by subsequent rumors and movements.   On September 5, having learned from the Mexican
papers that relations with the United States were strained,
and having heard the rumor that Mexico had ceded California to Great Britain for $7,000,000, considered that he
would be justified by the Monroe doctrine in seizing California in self-defence, thereby securing a prior claim of
conquest before Great Britain could obtain a claim by occupation.   Sailing to Monterey on October 19, acting on his
own authority, he took possession and ran up the United
States flag, but on the next day he restored the Mexican
standard.

Though Secretary Webster disavowed the exploit of

---

[9] Discovered by Captain Ingraham in 1791 and occupied by Captain Porter in 1813.   Occupied by the French in 1842.

Jones, the United States Government continued to contemplate the acquisition of the port of San Francisco by peaceable cession, and finally occupied it in the interests of civilization and future security, opening opportunities for American protective influence in Mexico, and giving a stimulus to communication with the Orient and Panama by lines of ocean steamers.

CHAPTER IV.

EARLY RELATIONS OF WHALERS AND TRADERS WITH THE NATIVES.

The islands of the Pacific have often been the scenes of thrilling disaster, romantic adventure, unbridled license, conflict, mutiny, treachery, and bloodshed. Along the track of the early whalers and traders, who carried with them the vices as well as the virtues of a higher civilization, were occasional shipwrecks, horrible massacres, and shocking indecencies. In cases of collision with the natives, the latter were not always the first offenders. Among the daring whaling captains, many of whom were scientific navigators, some were unprincipled, severe and indiscreet, and others were sometimes unable to control a crew so far removed from the arm of civil law.[1]

The crews were a motley collection of Indians, runaway slaves, renegade tars from the British navy, Irish, Dutch, and Hawaiians, as well as the shrewd natives of Massachusetts. The majority, like " Long Tom Coffin," were brave, hardy, intelligent sons of toil from New England's scant soil, who, by the offers of a share of the cargo, were induced to leave home and friends for a three-years' voyage, and to become alert and vigilant in their business. Sometimes a youth, who had worn out the forbearance of friends and tutors, left the counting-room or college for the novelty of an adventurous life on the broad ocean, where bones were sometimes broken and lives lost in rough contests with the mammoth spouting inhabitants of the deep.

---

[1] Cheever: Island World of the Pacific. C. S. Stewart: A Visit to the South Seas in the U. S. *Vincennes*, 1829-30. N. Y., 1831. J. N. Reynolds' Address, 1836.

Broils and mutinies occurred, but were usually put down. That, in 1823, on board the *Globe*, owned by a Nantucket firm, is the worst recorded.[2]

With Thomas Worth, commander, and twenty others, it left Edgarton December 20, 1822, sailed via Cape Horn and Hawaii to Japan seas, from which it returned to Hawaii with 550 barrels of oil. The crew had complained among themselves as to the irregularity of the meat supply. At Hawaii, six men deserted, and were replaced by five others, after which the vessel cruised toward Fanning's Island. The officers found frequent occasion to reprimand the new members, and caused one to be severely flogged. In January, 1824, one Comstock planned a mutiny and murdered the captain and mates. He ordered the third mate to be thrown overboard alive, and had his hands chopped off when he attempted to hold the ship. He then directed the ship via Kingsmill and Marshall's Island to the Mulgrave Islands, where he proposed to form a settlement. Here he joined a gang of natives, and, being suspected of treachery, was shot by Payne, one of his fellow-mutineers. Smith and six others, fearing Payne, escaped with the *Globe* to Valparaiso, where they were arrested by United States Consul Michael Hogan and sent to Nantucket. Payne, who, with nine others had been left at the Mulgraves, went into a paroxysm of rage when the absence of the vessel was discovered, but soon drowned his trouble by taking a native wife whom he had brought from another island, and his example was followed by others, who seemed to have had no fear of the natives. One morning, Payne, awakening and discovering that his wife was gone, grabbed muskets and started in search, found her, shot at her, flogged her severely, and put her in irons. His severities irritated the natives, who soon began to steal and to resist the restoration of articles. Probably because they were jealous of the

---

[2] Wm. Lay and C. M. Hussey: Narrative of a Mutiny on Board the *Globe*, New London, 1828.

chastity of their wives, the natives finally murdered all the whites except two, Lay and Hussey, who were saved only by the interposition of the natives, and were rescued in December, 1825, by Lieutenant Hiram Paulding, of the United States naval vessel *Dolphin*, which had made search by order of Secretary of the Navy.[3]

At Onavoora, in the Hawaiian group, which was a rendezvous for whale ships,[4] especially from January to April, many seamen, freed from a long confinement on board their vessels, often became so insubordinate and licentious that the captains were unable to restrict their propensities.   In some cases they threatened a riot unless the chiefs and missionaries should acquiesce in their demand for the repeal of the restrictions that deprived them of the society of females.[5] Even some of the crew of the United States ship *Dolphin*, in 1826, joined in opposition to missionaries.   Deserters were often secreted by the natives, and, in many cases, only to obtain the large rewards which captains offered for their return.

The Secretary of the Navy, seeing the extensive interests of the United States in every part of the Pacific, and having knowledge of the difficulties which not infrequently occurred in the neighborhood of many of the islands, considered the occasional presence of a public force very important.   During the South American revolt, the duties of the small squadron on the west coast of Chile and Peru, where American commerce was in danger from Spanish ves-

---

[3] Paulding: Cruise of the *Dolphin*.

[4] Honolulu became a depot for fresh supplies, repairs, and the temporary storage of whale oil.   As early as 1823, sometimes forty whaling vessels could be seen there on the same day.   The importance of the islands was recognized by the United States Government on September 19, 1820, when Secretary Monroe appointed John C. Jones as " Agent for Commerce and Seamen."

[5] In 1825 the chiefs of Hawaii issued a proclamation against women visiting vessels for immoral purposes, and crews tried to get missionaries to have it revoked.   Lieutenant Percival arrived on the *Dolphin*—protested against the decree and by threats induced the chiefs to rescind it.

sels, had prevented it from visiting the Society and Sandwich Islands, etc.   In 1825-6, the unsettled condition of the South American governments and the possibility that many from the former navy of Peru and Chile would resort to piracy, still exposed our commerce to dangers which seemed to require a " competent naval force " on the coast from Cape Horn to California.[6]   The need of a passage through the Isthmus of Panama was felt,[7] and in 1826, Captain Thomas ap Catesby Jones was ordered to go to the Hawaiian Islands to protect commerce, to relieve the islands of American seamen who had improperly deserted from whalers, to arrange to prevent desertions in the future, and to secure debts due American citizens.   He induced the sailors there to join ships in need of their services, and proceeded to negotiate [8] a treaty with the king (December 23, 1826) by which the latter agreed to permit trade, to aid wrecked vessels, to assist in preventing desertions, and, in time of war, to protect United States ships and citizens, in the Hawaiian Islands, against all our enemies.[9]   He found that the British consul and influential foreigners and shipmasters were against the missionaries.[10]

American commerce in the Pacific was at this time augmenting very rapidly.   In 1826 there were 2000 seamen at Honolulu alone, and, for their protection, the Secretary of the Navy, in December, 1827, recommended that six vessels be kept in commission in the Pacific.[11]   By 1828 there was no longer any fear of our commerce being molested by Spanish ships, and the Navy Department hoped that our armed vessels might frequently visit the Society, Sandwich and other islands most frequented by our merchant ships.

---

[6] Rp. Secy. of Navy, Dec., 1826.

[7] H. Res., Dec., 1825.   Naval Com. Rp., Jan., 1826.

[8] Ruschenberger: Voyage Around the World, 1836-37, chapter iv.

[9] Though this treaty, or convention was never ratified by the United States it continued to be a tacit understanding.

[10] Rev. J. M. Alexander: Islands of the Pacific, chap. vii.

[11] Rp. Secy. of Navy, Dec. 1, 1827.

In 1829 it was estimated that in one year Hawaii was visited by 100 American vessels with cargoes valued at $5,000,-
000. American merchants were seeking to increase trade
with the Orient, and to secure a greater protection from the
American Government.

In 1829 Captain Finch, with the United States ship *Vincennes,* was sent by the American Government to endeavor
to improve our relations in the Pacific.[12] He visited
Nukuhiva [of the Washington Islands], and, through William Morrison, as an interpreter, who was collecting sandalwood there, endeavored to persuade the chiefs to stop
the civil wars which arose from tribal jealousies, and often
from some mere petty theft, insult or misunderstanding.
He explained that our purpose was good-will and peace,
and that our vessels fought only those who ill-treated our
defenceless trading vessels.[13]

Passing on to Tahiti, where natives were less rude and
naked than the Nukuhivans, he saw several white persons,
attended a mission church, and found that since 1821 the
island had been governed by a code of laws (and penalties)
including trial by jury. Finding the seventeen-year-old
Queen Pamaré I. at work (September 1, 1829), he alluded
to the recent conduct of herself and the regent toward some
deserters from an American whaler, and, after the diplomatic attempt of the regent to screen herself and the queen,
he pleasantly dismissed the subject in a manner calculated
to prevent a recurrence of such conduct. Several secondary
chiefs made short speeches expressing pleasure as to the
purpose and the manner of the visit, and the queen sent a
letter to President Jackson, saying: "Continue to sail
your vessels without suspicion. Our harbors are good and
our refreshments abundant."

---

[12] C. S. Stewart: A Visit to the South Seas.
[13] In his reports, Finch said that for the convenience of the
United States the situation of Nukuhiva was more convenient than
Oahu or the Society Islands—unless a canal should be cut through
the Isthmus.

Conditions at Hawaii caused the missionaries to welcome the arrival of the *Vincennes* and Captain Finch, as well as Chaplain C. S. Stewart, who had been a missionary there in 1822-5. Unfortunately, the merchants and the missionaries were at loggerheads, the missionaries saying that Americans, and other foreigners, had been guilty of bad conduct on the islands, and had opposed all efforts of the religious teachers, and that on the slightest pretext the foreign officials threatened vengeance upon the " timid and peace-loving rulers," who had accepted the decalogue as their only code of laws. On the other hand, the foreign residents (merchants) complained that the government was controlled by the missionaries, and was unsatisfactory. Finch saw at Oahu many indications of irregularities in commerce, severity to crews, and bad effects of desertions. Consul Jones, speaking (October 30, 1829) of the growing importance of the Sandwich Islands to the increasing American trades, said there should be semi-annual visits of United States war vessels to reduce desertions and mutinies, and to punish the guilty.

At a reception given by King Kanikeaouli, Captain Finch presented him with maps and books, and read him a friendly message from the President,[14] assuring him that the United States desired to preserve his sovereign rights, and sent war vessels for protection only where native governments failed to protect. Capt. Finch advised him to prevent the secretion of deserters, to liquidate his debts, to cease competing with private individuals in the tavern business, to spend his time usefully, to learn English, and to hold semi-annual meetings of his chiefs to revise state affairs. He stated that United States citizens violating the laws should be censured.

American merchants and traders, residing at Oahu, protested against communication with the king by the Secretary of the Navy instead of through the regular channels

---

[14] Laura Fish Judd: Honolulu, etc., N. Y., 1880.

of the State Department. They denied that American citizens had been guilty of bad conduct on the island, declared that the United States would have no cognizance of offences committed beyond the limits of its jurisdiction, and insinuated that the *Vincennes* had done nothing but aid in saddling a religion on the " ignorant and unsuspecting islanders."

The king wrote to President Jackson (November 23, 1829) thanking him for the maps and globes and hoping for perfect agreement. The chiefs, in a conference with Finch, acknowledged that they owed American merchants $50,000 and pledged themselves to pay it in nine months.[15]

During the next few years there were still other sources of dispute at Hawaii. The king, who had charged no tax or rent to foreigners, feared that by leasing land he would run the risk of losing control over the islands, and claimed the right to prevent American citizens from selling or otherwise transferring their houses, stating that they reverted to him when they passed from the original owner. In 1836 Commodore E. P. Kennedy, of the United States ship *Peacock*, opened negotiations with the king as to subjects of dispute, but no agreement was reached.[16]

Captain Benjamin Morrell, of the *Antarctic*, who sailed from New York September, 1829, leaving his wife at Manila (with the wife of an English merchant), in April, 1830, started on a trip to the Fijis, and has left us an interesting narrative of his relations with the natives of Williams (c. 5° N., 153° E.), Monteverdeson's, Massacre and Bergh's Islands, and of islands discovered by him north and east of New Guinea. At Williams Island, while the girls were bringing him wreaths of wild flowers and receiving beads, other natives were lurking in the bushes ready for a treacherous attack. At the Monteverdeson's Islands, the natives

---

[15] Stewart: Visit to South Seas, vol. ii, p. 212.
[16] Ruschenberger: Voyage Around the World, 1836-37, pp. 498-502.

brought cocoanuts and bread fruit, and those who wore
clothes (the married) stripped it all off to trade for old knives
and beads, but some were preparing to make an attack in
canoes, and Morrell said he left to prevent slaughtering
them. At the Massacre Islands Morrell made a treaty of
amity and commerce with King Nero, but soon after beginning to erect a house and plant garden seeds, he saw signs
of treachery, thieving and dissimulation, and later, sixteen
of his men were killed while making a desperate defence.
The natives suffered a heavier loss, and Morrell, after going
to Manila for more men, returned in September to admin-
ister a wholesale chastisement. With "eloquent cannon,"
he repulsed a flotilla of the natives, and then, after quieting
those of the excited crew who wanted to depopulate the
island, he purchased with cutlery a small island (Wallace's)
and landed seventy men to cure bêche-de-mer. On September 18, he repulsed several hundred yelling natives that
invaded the island, but being still harassed from time to
time, he did not wait to complete his cargo, but burned his
houses and bade adieu to the crowds of inhospitable
islanders who had eaten the whites they had killed, and had
apparently never suffered any bad effects. After visiting
other islands north and east of New Guinea, where he obtained two natives, Morrell returned to New York via
Manila, Singapore and the Cape of Good Hope, and in
1832 published an account of his voyages, claimed that he
had discovered a group of islands where a great opportunity
was waiting for the advance of enterprise, and encouraged
the fitting out of a good vessel with a crew of young men.[17]

In March, 1834, T. J. Jacobs, aged 16, and just out of
college, joined a small trading expedition to the Pacific in
the clipper *Margaret Oakley*, of which Morrell was captain.
The expedition proved to be principally one of adventure,
exploration and romance in the region of Papua (New

---

[17] Capt. Benj. Morrell: Narrative of Four Voyages, 1821-31,
N. Y., 1832.

Guinea), Bidera (New Britain) and the picturesque Admiralty Islands. Trade was opened with well-armed savages, beads and pictures were given to the girls and young women who came to the vessel in canoes, and interest was taken in watching the natives in their love-making and their daily sea-bath. Some of the crew would have been willing to remain in this rural, romantic land of paradise, whose simple-hearted people sometimes besought them not to go. Jacobs, whom the prince and several women tried to induce to marry and settle on their island, wrote: "I felt strongly tempted to embark forthwith, in company with several shipmates, for the uninhabited island of Garone, in the Morrell group, and colonize the beautiful bay. At present it was impracticable; but at another time the captain intended to return with a party of young men and women from the United States for that purpose." In 1844 he was still contemplating a trading and colonizing expedition to that quarter, which he considered to be "exceedingly inviting." The *Oakley*, during her voyage, reached the vicinity of Norfolk Island, which had been uninhabited when visited by Captain Cook, in 1774, but was now a penal colony for life convicts—for those of a worse class than were banished to Sydney (Botany Bay). She then sailed through the Sulu straits and traded at Sulu harbor, passed the mouth of Manila bay and exchanged cargo below Canton. Morrell, stating that the romance of the voyage was ended, dismissed many of the crew and started to return to New York, but probably engaged in some enterprise in the South Seas.[18]

Many Americans suffered shipwreck, privation and death in the Fijis. About 1827, the *Oeno* of Nantucket, was shipwrecked there, and most of the crew were massacred. In 1830 an English vessel brought news that a young lad, whose widowed mother lived at Nantucket, was still alive on one of the islands. Captain Coffin and part of the crew

---

[18] T. J. Jacobs: Scenes, Incidents and Adventures in the Pacific Ocean. N. Y., 1844.

of the *Awaskonks* were murdered on the islands a short time later, and the brig *Fawn*, of Salem, Massachusetts, was lost there in 1830. In the same year the *Glide*, owned by Joseph Peabody, of Salem, struck a rock and sprung a leak, and after going to Manila for repairs, returned to trade and soon found it necessary to retaliate on natives by driving them to the mountains and destroying some of their canoes.[19] The king seemed friendly, and rebuilt drying houses destroyed by his hostile natives, but after his retirement to his town, thirty miles in the interior, the *Glide* found it convenient to leave, and was wrecked near by in a storm. A chief claimed the wreck, and the natives were soon laden with plunder. The officers and crew seemed to enjoy the life on the island, amidst bounteous fruit, festival and entertainment. They (16) were finally carried by the *Harriet* (which arrived from New York May 22, 1831) to Wallis Island, which they said had a beautiful climate, plentiful fruits and hospitable natives. Arriving soon after at Oahu, where American missions had been established since 1820, some of them, reflecting that missions accomplished more good than warriors " armed to the teeth," stated that the Fijians could be improved like the Hawaiians and Samoans.[20]

In many instances unfortunate seamen were held as captives by the islanders. In 1833, A. S. Joy, of Nantucket, learned that there were white prisoners on the Tonga and also on the Navigators' Islands. On July 30, 1830, twenty-two young men, excited with the hope of seeing distant regions and bettering their fortunes from the treasures of the deep, left New Bedford in the *Monitor*, under com-

---

[19] When the *Glide* (in November, 1830) stopped at Overlau, of the Fijis, David Whelpy, who had been an American chieftain there since deserting a whale ship from Nantucket several years before, was on friendly terms with the King of Bau, and seemed to have great influence over the natives.

[20] W. G. Dix and James Oliver: Wreck of the *Glide*, with Recollections of Fiji and Wallis Island. N. Y., 1848.

mand of Captain E. C. Barnard. They rounded the Cape of Good Hope and started for one of the Ladrones, but after much bad weather, their vessel struck on a coral reef off Pelew Islands, nearly 1000 miles east of the Philippines, and was lost. The survivors were detained by the natives, and through the influence of an Englishman, who had deserted his vessel twenty years before, and was now a kind of chief, they lived a life of ease and plenty for six months; but tiring of the place, they escaped to North's Island, where they were attacked. Captain Barnard and one other returned to New York to tell the story of their adventure.

The news of the capture and plunder of the *Friendship*, of Salem, Massachusetts, at Quallah Battoo on the coast of Sumatra (where she was engaged in the pepper trade) on February 9, 1831, induced the United States Government to take prompt action for securing better protection for American sailors and commerce along the coasts and on the islands of the Far East.[21] The United States frigate *Potomac* was immediately sent to investigate, and being able to obtain no satisfactory negotiations, proceeded to retaliate by attacking the town. The American troops silently disembarked after midnight, firing soon began, and notwithstanding the hard fighting of the whooping natives, in which even women participated, the Malays were defeated and the American colors in a few hours waved over their forts.[22] Captain Downs, in making peace, informed the natives that if they perpetrated any more outrages they would be punished again. J. N. Reynolds, who went with the expedition, urged that a few instances of prompt retaliation would have a good effect by impressing nations with our power. Sailing home via Oahu, he learned from a letter of Consul J. C. Jones to Captain Downs, that persons from nearly all the whalers caused trouble to the captains by at-

---

[21] President Jackson's Message, Dec. 6, 1831.
[22] Francis Warriner: Cruise of the U. S. Frigate *Potomac* round the World, 1831-34, N. Y., 1835. J. N. Reynolds: Voyage of the *Potomac*, 1831-34, N. Y., 1835.

tempts at mutiny or desertion, and afterwards became outlaws on shore. He believed that some of the causes of abuse in the whale fleets could be reached only by the strong arm of the United States Government, and advocated that, besides regular visits of war vessels, the number of consuls should be increased and that they should receive regular salaries.[23]

Observing our increasing interests at Valparaiso and northward, and looking westward to the new and extensive island world, Reynolds said the vast Pacific was, by force of events, becoming an ocean in which the Americans were immediately interested, and would probably be the theatre of our future sea fights. He urged the necessity of a government exploring expedition to the South Seas, greater protection to trade, and the establishment of safe harbors.

Soon after the dispatch of the *Potomac* to Sumatra, the Jackson administration, in view of the fact that the United States had no colonial establishments, felt the necessity of securing ports in the vicinity of Borneo, Siam and Japan, at which American vessels might always be received and protected, and sent Edmund Roberts with instructions (1832) to negotiate for treaties for the safety of seamen and commerce.[24] Soon the project for a United States exploring expedition to the Pacific, proposed long before, was revived, and the Government was finally induced to undertake it.

---

[23] The *Potomac*, stopping at the Galapagos group, carried the news to J. Vilomil, a native of Louisiana, that he had been appointed consul at Guayaquil but he could not be induced to accept it. See page 60.

[24] I Sp. M., 52.

CHAPTER V.

THE UNITED STATES EXPLORING EXPEDITION,[1] 1839-43.

During the first half century of her existence, though her vessels sailed around the globe, and European powers were planting colonies and making explorations on far-off shores, the United States did not adopt any systematic effort to obtain geographical knowledge in the Pacific where American enterprise and commerce had been extending so rapidly. It was a period of internal development; but the importance of pointing out harbors and paths for seamen in the Pacific was gradually learned from the school of experience.

From the earliest times the desire to secure a lucrative trade was not the only motive which induced men to sail on long journeys to the distant seas. Some sought adventure and romance, and others were urged by the desire to discover new fields of activity. In the spring of 1812, President Madison took steps to aid an expedition under Captain Edward Fanning to make explorations in the South Seas and voyage around the world, but the enterprise was abandoned on account of the opening of the war with England.[2] In September, 1817, the *Sea Fox* sailed from New York to the New South Shetlands and Palmer's Land.[3]

---

[1] Charles Wilkes: The U. S. Exploring Expedition. 5 vols. Phila., 1845. [Subsequently, eleven additional volumes were published.]

[2] H. Doc. 57, 26-1, vol. ii.

[3] Captain Briscoe, of London, in 1832, observed an island 67° 15' south latitude, 69° 29' west longitude, which he took possession of in the name of William IV. and called Adelaide Island, in honor of the English queen. Commenting on this act, Captain

In 1822 Captain Benjamin Morrell sailed to the Antarctic seas in the *Wasp*. Reaching 70° 14', he resolved to make an appeal to the United States Government for countenance and assistance to enable him to go farther. " To the only free nation on the earth," said he, " should belong the glory of exploring a spot of the globe which is the *ne plus ultra* of latitude." [4] Fanning was confident that vessels could reach the South Pole, and in 1829-30 he was in charge of the brigs *Seraph* and *Annawan* on an " infant expedition " to the South Seas. [5]

In 1826, John N. Reynolds, a native of Ohio, and a congressman (who went with the *Annawan* expedition as far as the west coast of South America), had proposed the project of a Pacific and Polar expedition under the auspices of the Government. [6] His idea was seconded by citizens of Nantucket and other New England seaports, and by the legislatures of seven States. The Maryland House of Delegates, mentioning the enterprise of other nations in acquiring geographical knowledge, extending their influence, and opening new channels of commerce, asserted that the United States, after its success in the stu-

---

Morrell said: " But these lands were visited fifteen years ago by our sealers and taken possession of in the name of our sovereign, the people; and when a true record shall be made . . . the name of Adelaide Island must be changed . . . . We have a long running, unsettled account in this matter of giving names to places, with some of our neighbors, which we may as well begin to have posted up, for the purpose of preventing future disputes. . . . Our hardy seamen feel able even to cast anchor on that point where all the meridians terminate, where our flag may be unfurled and left to wave." [J. N. Reynolds' Address, 1836.]

[4] Capt. Benj. Morrell: A Narrative of Four Voyages to the South Sea, etc., 1822-31, N. Y., 1832.

[5] Edward Fanning: Voyages Around the World, etc., 1792-1832.

[6] During the summer of 1828 Reynolds had obtained data from whaling captains of New London, Newport, Nantucket, etc., and from their log-books, showing that 200 American vessels were engaged in whaling and seal fisheries, capturing about 8000 whales each year, and that our enterprising seamen had often discovered rocks, reefs, and islands, and in many cases had given valuable information to European chart makers.

pendous experiment of self-government in politics, with its increasing population and commercial relations and interest coextensive with the civilized world, could afford to enter into the " interesting and extensive field for enterprise in the Southern hemisphere," and offered a resolution that " a polar expedition could scarcely fail in adding something to the general stock of national wealth and knowledge, and to the honor and glory of the United States." [7]   Other petitions or memorials urged that the American industry in the Pacific having increased the wealth of our country, and furnished a nursery for bold and hardy seamen, as well as a source of employment and human comforts, had made intercourse with the Pacific a matter of public interest and should be encouraged by the survey of islands and coasts.[8]

In January and February, 1828, the subject was brought before Congress by executive documents, and on May 21 a resolution of the House requested the President to send one or more small vessels to the Pacific and South Seas to examine coasts, islands and reefs, and ascertain their location. The Secretary of the Navy selected the *Peacock*, and in November, 1828, suggested the purchase of another vessel and the selection of instruments and scientific men.

In February, 1829, the House still urged the expedition, and the Secretary of the Navy, in a document sent to that body, stated that the object was to examine islands and coasts, " both known and unknown," as far south as circumstances, safety and prudence would permit explorations, and that an additional appropriation would be needed.[9]

The Senate, to which the House resolution had never been submitted, feeling that the expedition would be expensive and was related to the foreign policy, favored delay and investigation, and hoped that the Secretary of the Navy

[7] H. Exec. Doc. 88, 20-1, vol. iii, Jan. 22, 1828.
[8] H. Exec. Docs. 179 and 201, 20-1, vol. v, Feb. and March. 1828.
[9] Sen. Exec. Doc. 77, 20-2, Feb. 16, 1829.

would never again feel justified to act upon the resolution of the House alone. The Senate committee, considering the wide unsettled and unexplored regions at home, saw nothing in the condition of the United States to recommend distant voyages of exploration, and feared that the discovery of countless islands or new continents might result in the evils of adventure, visionary hopes and large emigration, tending to urge us " to plant the American standard on soil discovered by American enterprise," and, perhaps, to establish distant and expensive colonies, " which could only be defended at an expense not to be estimated, and which could not be taken under the protection of the United States without an abandonment of the fundamental principles of our policy, and a departure from those wise and prudent maxims which have hitherto restrained us from forming unnecessary connexions abroad."

The majority of the committee thought that before venturing upon a premature expedition to distant seas, where even to survey the 200 known islands would be a large undertaking, the Government should make accurate surveys of our coasts. Though they held that the opening of new sources to commerce, as well as agriculture, might safely be left to the enterprise and instinctive sagacity of individuals, they favored a small expedition to make surveys in the track of our vessels in the Pacific.[10]

After sailing to the Pacific and circumnavigating the globe, Reynolds returned to the United States in 1834, and prepared to renew his project in Congress. Collecting information which he had received from the whalers,[11] he proposed exploration on both sides of the equator from South America to Asia, and southward beyond previous discoveries. (Captain Cook had been stopped by ice at 68° south latitude, but Captain Palmer and other Americans had

---

[10] Sen. Rp. 94, 20-2, Feb. 23, 1829. Mrs. A. E. Carrell, on the " First American Exploring Expedition," in Harper's Mag., vol. xliv, Dec., 1871.

[11] Exec. Doc. 105, 23-2, Jan. 24, 1835.

gone beyond that in search of furs and seals.)   J. Q. Adams
led the House in favor of the expedition, and an act of Congress, May 14, 1835, authorized it.   Many thought the
expedition should be scientific, and that it might throw
some light on the source of the American aborigines. Some
opposed the enterprise on the ground that it was an eastern
measure, and a visionary one.[12]   Hawes, of Kentucky (May
5, 1836) compared it to the establishment of light-houses in
the skies, and said, if it passed, he expected a proposition
for a voyage to the moon next.   Others urged that it was
for the general interest.   Though Jackson favored the expedition, his Secretary of the Navy, Dickerson, did not,
and during the three years of preparation Russia sent out
three expeditions.

Reynolds continued to urge that the United States should
increase our knowledge of the Pacific[13] in order to render
less hazardous the voyages of our hardy sailors upon the
rock-chafed billows of seas only partially explored, and in
unfrequented bays of barbarous natives.   Of the coast of
Sumatra, where many of our vessels sailed and where we
had recently sent the *Potomac* to punish the natives who had
captured the American *Friendship*, we had no charts; nor
had we any of the Fijis, where several of our ships had been
lost and men slaughtered.   In the vicinity of the Society,
New Caledonia and Solomon's Islands, where we had over
200 whale ships, there was much danger of shipwreck.   The
stories of lost mariners were not fictions.   Almost every
arrival from the Pacific[14] brought some news of shipwreck,
mutiny or massacre.   Even at the Friendly Islands captains had been seized in order to exact ransoms, and the
presence of a man-of-war seemed to be necessary to protect seamen who had never received any bounties, but who,
as children of the sea, might be called to bear a double share

[12] Cong. Globe, May 9, 1836.
[13] J. N. Reynolds' Address, Apr. 3, 1836.
[14] In 1837 it was estimated that the United States had 460 vessels
in the Pacific. This was one-tenth of all our tonnage.

of usefulness in some great ocean conflict of the future. The United States squadron on the Pacific coasts at this time consisted only of one frigate, two sloops and a schooner. Reynolds considered that a judicious exhibition of a stronger force, together with a humane policy, was necessary to gain the confidence of the natives.[15]

Those who urged the expedition proposed that it should have the following purposes:[16]

1. To note accurately the position of islands and harbors and rocks along the paths of United States whalers and traders.

2. To release from the islands unhappy captives left there by wrecks.

3. To suppress misconduct on American vessels, prevent mutiny and desertions, and endeavor to end cruelty, licentiousness and extortion in the islands.

4. Look for land in the South polar seas.

5. Collect specimens and facts to subserve the advancement of science in natural history, linguistics, etc.

Leaders in Navy Department circles held that it would encroach upon the rights of naval officers for a corps of scientific citizens to accompany the expedition. Many obstacles were presented to defeat the object of the enterprise. The people were told that it would be expensive, confer no benefit upon commerce, and that it aimed at nothing but to explore Antarctic icebergs. The Navy Department decided Reynolds should not accompany the expedition, and taking advantage of the crisis of 1837, convoked a

---

[15] On June 11, 1836, Benjamin Rodman, of New Bedford, in a letter to J. N. Reynolds, referring to the advantages which the expedition would have upon our marine colonies, said: "Why should we have governors, judges, and all the paraphernalia of courts in territories where there is a bare possibility that an Indian may be murdered, or become a murderer, steal a horse or have his horse stolen; and not have a superintending influence abroad, where our ships are daily traversing from island to island . . . . that the savage may be awed into respect, and the mutineer's hand bound in submission?"   [16] N. Am. Rev., Oct., 1837.

new commission to cut down the force. Jones, who was
to have commanded the expedition, resigned; Shubrick declined to take his place; Kearney was prevented from accepting the command; Captain Gregory, being a friend of
Reynolds, declined, and Wilkes, who had been in Europe
making purchases of instruments, was appointed over the
heads of his fellow-officers.

The expedition was finally organized in 1838.[17] Its purpose was purely " scientific and useful," though several
scientific men were not permitted to sail with it.[18] It was
divested of all military character, the armament being
adopted merely for necessary defence against natives, while
engaged in surveys, and not adopted with views of conquest
or war. There were six vessels in the squadron:[19]

The *Vincennes*, sloop-of-war ....780 tons
"   *Peacock*, sloop-of-war..........650 "
"   *Porpoise*, gun-brig ....230 "
"   *Relief*, slow-going store ship.
"   *Sea Gull*, New York pilot-boat..110 " } tenders.
"   *Flying Fish*, New York pilot-boat. 96 " }

Wilkes was directed by his instructions to determine the
longitude of Rio Janeiro, examine the resources of Rio
Negro, make researches at Terra del Fuego, explore the
South Antarctic between Powell's group and Palmer's Land,
sail to Cook's *ne plus ultra* in 105 west longitude, return to
Valparaiso for supplies, visit the Society Islands, verify the
position of certain shoals in the Navigators' group, examine
the Fijis with a view to the selection of a harbor for whaling
vessels, go to Sydney and from there make a second
attempt to penetrate within the Antarctic circle south of Van
Dieman's Land, and after returning to the Sandwich Islands
for more stores, to explore along the Columbia river and

---

[17] Exec. Doc. 147, 25-2, vol. vii, Feb. 5, 1838. 630 pp. with good
alphabetical index.
[18] For the sake of harmony, Reynolds was not allowed to go.
[19] Exec. Doc. 255, 25-2, vol. viii, Mar. 16, 1838.

California, then direct his course to Japan, endeavor to find a safe route through the Sulu sea which would shorten the route of our vessels to China during the season of contrary monsoons (and facilitate our navigation with the Philippines) and return to the United States via the Straits of Billiton, Singapore, and the Cape of Good Hope.[20]

Before reaching the Pacific Wilkes stopped at Madeira, made a brief stay at St. Iago, of the Cape Verde group, and remained at Rio six weeks for repairs and to replace inferior supplies. The passage around Cape Horn was dangerous and the *Sea Gull* was lost. On April 14 the *Relief* reached Valparaiso. In May the *Vincennes* and *Peacock* arrived. The squadron next stopped in Callao, the harbor of Lima. The *Relief* then went to the Sandwich Islands and to Sydney carrying supplies. Wilkes, with other vessels, went to the Poumotu group (Low Archipelago or Tuomata). A month later he reached Minerva Island (Clermont Tonnerre) of the same group and began the study of corals. The few natives seen gave no welcome, and apparently did not want to be discovered. " Go to your lands," said they, " this belongs to us and we do not want to have anything to do with you."

Tahiti, where Cook observed the transit of Venus in 1769, was the next rendezvous. American, British and French consuls lived there (also missionaries), and whaling vessels often came for supplies. The natives brought a profusion of pigs, cocoanuts and bananas. Owing to the clamorous press of natives, only *great* chiefs were permitted to come aboard.[21] The latter came to solicit laundry work. While surveys were being made the scientists studied the geological formations of the island. Wilkes found it necessary to protest against illicit trade and excessive use of intoxicants.

---

[20] Synopsis of the Wilkes Expedition, Washington, 1842.

[21] Women were not allowed to come on the ship at night, as they had evidently been accustomed to do with other vessels.

After a visit to Eimeo, Wilkes sailed to the Samoan Islands and surveyed and mapped them as he had Tahiti. At Oloosinga he dined with the king, and not understanding Samoan etiquette, came near creating a disturbance by showing the same courtesy to a kanaka (common) as he did to the king. He surveyed Pango Pango harbor, of Tutuila, and the Bay of Apia, of Upolu. The council of chiefs of the Malo party, in the presence of the naval officers and missionaries (November 5, 1839), agreed to rules and regulations for protection of foreign consuls, vessels and seamen, the apprehension of deserters, prohibition of all trade in spirituous liquors, and all work on Sunday, except when absolutely necessary, and regulating landing anchorage and pilotage. For a dangerous renegade that the United States desired, a large reward was offered.

From Apia, Wilkes sailed to Sydney via Fijis, and after examining into social problems and penal colonies, prepared to explore in the polar ice-fields. Leaving the scientific corps, he started on a voyage of two and one-half months, and on January 16, 1840, discovered land within the Antarctic circle.[22] After completing repairs at Sydney, he went to New Zealand and witnessed native war dances, but was not interested in what he saw there. On reaching the Tonga (Friendly) group he found the natives quarrelling and trying to annex neighbors' territory, and he attempted to reconcile the parties.

At the Fijis, where he lost two officers through the treacherous character of the cannibalistic natives, he obtained (June 10, 1840) the signatures of eleven kings and chiefs to the agreement concerning rules and regulations previously accepted by Samoan chiefs.[23]

At the Sandwich Islands (October, 1840) he received information from the United States. He was impressed

---

[22] U. S. Exploring Expedition, vol. ii, chaps. ix and x.
[23] G. M. Colvocoresses: Four years in a Government Expedition, 1838-42. N. Y., 1852.

with the good influence of the missionaries in the transformation of the natives. After a brief rest, the *Vincennes*
and *Porpoise* were directed toward the coast of Oregon, and
the *Peacock* sailed to the Phoenix group, Samoa, Ellice and
Kingsmill groups, and then via Honolulu to the Oregon
coast, where it was wrecked.[24]

Returning to Hawaii in October, 1841, Wilkes sailed to
Manila [25] and made observations in the interior of Luzon.
Of the Sulu sea he made surveys and charts, and, at Sohung,
obtained a treaty (a promise) from the Sultan, guaranteeing
protection to all United States vessels visiting his dominion.
Reaching Singapore in February, 1842, he sailed home via
Cape of Good Hope, with a cargo of plants and seeds, from
the South Seas, which formed the nucleus of the Botanical
Gardens at Washington.

Soon after his return to the United States, Wilkes was
arraigned before a court-martial on charges of oppression,
injustice to his men, illegal and severe punishment of merciless savages, falsehood and scandalous conduct, but he was
acquitted after an investigation of six weeks.[26] In his own
report of the expedition, Wilkes said: "I shall always
have the proud and conscientious feeling of having done
my duty; and that I have carried the moral influence of our
country wherever our flag has waved."

The Wilkes expedition was followed by exploring expeditions to other parts of the world: Lynch to the Dead
sea, Fremont to California, and Dr. Kane to the Arctic
regions. The second national enterprise by the United
States in the Pacific was undertaken in 1853, under the
direction of Commander Cadwallader Ringgold, and its
purpose was to make explorations and meteorological observations in Behring sea, the Japan sea, the Yellow sea,

---

[24] U. S. Exploring Expedition, vol. v.

[25] His report of the expedition gives a summary of the history
of Manila.

[26] Navy Dept. Tracts, vol. xiv, No. 25. Wilkes: Antarctic Exploration. [Letter to Washington Union, Aug. 12, 1847.]

and the Japan, Kurile, Aleutian and Bonin Islands [27] in the interests of commerce, and for the welfare and protection of the many American citizens who were engaged in the whale fisheries. It consisted of five vessels: the *Vincennes,* the steamer *John Hancock,* the brig *Porpoise,* the tender *J. Fenimore Cooper,* and the *John P. Kennedy.* Important surveys in the North Pacific were conducted under the command of John Rodgers[28] The increasing importance of South America, the interesting islands to the westward, and California and Oregon, induced the Secretary of the Navy, in December, 1856, to recommend that the regular Pacific force should be supplemented by a second squadron.[29]

---

[27] F. D. Stuart: Journal of a cruise of the U. S. Ship *Vincennes.* [In MS. at Navy Department.]

[28] Rep. of Secy. of Navy, Dec. 3, 1855. Lieut. A. W. Habersham: My Last Cruise. Phila., 1857.

[29] In 1855, the regular Pacific squadron cruised in the vicinity of Astoria, Hawaii, Fiji, Mexico, and Chile. In December, 1855, the Secretary of the Navy announced that a vessel would soon be sent to correct irregularities of the natives in the Marquesas group.

CHAPTER VI.

COLONIAL ESTABLISHMENTS.

THE PORT LLOYD COLONY IN THE BONIN ISLANDS.

Among the many American pioneers in the Pacific who for over a century, with silent and persevering efforts, have led in a movement of whose magnitude they scarcely dreamed, there were some who long ago had views of establishing settlements or securing advantageous stations on islands in the Far East.[1] Delano, who sailed from Boston

---

[1] Others were interested in establishments on islands nearer to the American coast of the Pacific.

In 1813, Captain D. Porter, asserting American rights by discovery, conquest and possession, and "influenced by humanity" and the request of the friendly natives, as well as by views of national policy, and the immediate need of security and supplies for his vessels, formally took possession of Madison Island, of the Washington group, and took steps to hold it.

In 1832, Governor J. Vilomil, a native of Louisiana, established on Charles Island, of the Galapagos group, a colony which he had long projected. In 1811, he thought of applying to Spain for permission to make the settlement, but heard that Spain would probably not permit it. When Colombia established its independence he again contemplated his colony, but his friends discouraged him and kept him inactive until 1820 when, influenced by the death of his wife and two children, and tired of society, he petitioned for a charter which, granted in 1831, conceded the possession of the islands and authorized the establishment of a colony. Colonel Hernandez and twelve colonists who, in January, 1832, were sent to take possession, were followed in April and June by both men and women, and, in October, by Governor Vilomil and eighty others. They labored with zeal, and soon the productions of the island were enough for several hundred more inhabitants. Governor Vilomil, who, seated upon his rock, exercised almost absolute power, under the severest penalties prohibited the introduction of liquors, and administered severe punishments when they were considered necessary to teach the colonists that their true

as second officer on the *Massachusetts,* March, 1790, left
the vessel at Macao and entered English service under Commodore McClure, who planned and began a romantic project of making an establishment on the Pelew Islands.

In 1834 Captain Morrell visited some small islands of the
Admiralty and other groups, which he had intentions of
colonizing with a party of young men and women from the
United States.[2]

In 1832, five white persons,[3] with a small party of natives,
sailed from the Sandwich Islands to establish a colony on
Peel Island, one of the uninhabited, picturesque Bonin
group, 500 miles from Japan. Having tried and become
tired of various climes, they sighed for a far-off isolated
island where they "could love as they loved in the golden
time." They had been informed by Charlton, the British
consul, that the islands had waters abounding in fish and
turtle, woods full of game, shores with safe harbors, and
fertile valleys green with verdure and capable of yielding
rich returns. On reaching Port Lloyd with their stock
and garden seeds, and the British flag, they found that they
had been misled, but saw that it was too late to return. The
beautiful scenery—bays, valleys, ravines, natural tunnels,
and wide-spreading trees—were attractive, but Mazarra saw
nothing to invite permanent settlement, and his party soon
found that in this Far West men must work, and that waters
reflecting the bright stars on silent nights were frequently
tossed by typhoons, earthquakes and irregular winds.

---

interests were peace among themselves and justice towards the
people of visiting vessels. Though appointed United States consul
at Guayaquil, he declined the position, stating that he could be of
more service as governor of his colony, and that his enterprise
would be valuable to at least one branch of American commerce.
J. N. Reynolds visited the island in 1833 and said it might soon
become very important to the whaling interests of the United
States in the Pacific where a new and extensive world was opening to the people of the West.

[2] See p. 45.

[3] They were: Matthew Mazarra, a Genoese; A. B. Chapman and
Nathaniel Savory, of Massachusetts; Richard Millechamp, of England; and Charles Johnson, of Denmark.

The group had been discovered as early as 1675 by the Japanese. In 1823, Captain Coffin, of the American whaler *Transit*, had visited one of the islands and given his name to it. An English whaler, *William*, had visited the harbor in 1826 and was lost by neglect. In 1827, Captain Beechey, of the British vessel *Blossom*, had taken possession of Peel Island. The convenient intermediary position of the group for watching the trade with China, the Philippines and Russia was not fully seen at that day.

The settlers built snugly thatched, comfortable cabins and prepared to furnish supplies for passing whalers, but their life was by no means peaceful. Dissensions arose. The whaler *Cadmus*, in 1833, left fifteen refractory seamen, who defiantly committed outrages. In 1836 the settlers agreed to a written code called " The laws of the Bonin Islands," which was posted on the wall of the dwelling of Mr. Chapin, who had a library of fifty or sixty books and was characterized as polite and intelligent. This code provided that all disputes should be settled by the opinion of the majority; that none should sell turtle or aid vessels in getting it; that none should maltreat another's slaves or servants or endeavor to seduce any woman from her lord; and that none should encourage or aid desertions from ships. Later in the same year, an American vessel on a voyage around the world, stopped at the settlement. Ruschenberger has given us a picture of the people at the time. There were then nineteen women on the island. The morality of the community was of a low grade, and religion was out of the question. Infanticide and infidelity were common. Both men and women lounged on rough-hewn logs in the shade, abandoning all work and devoting their time to the consumption of three barrels of New England rum which had just been received, the first they had had for nearly a year.[4]

After Millechamp returned to England, the task of gov-

---

[4] Ruschenberger: Voyage Around the World, 1836-37. Chap. xli. Phila.. 1838.

erning the little colony devolved upon Mazarra, who, in 1842, returned to the Sandwich Islands in an English whaler to encourage additional settlers and laborers to emigrate. He also obtained from Alexander Simpson, the British consul, such recognition as he felt necessary to establish his authority. Though there were then only twenty persons in the small colony, he had found it no easy matter to govern. Simpson drew up a paper requesting that Mazarra should be considered the head of the colony until he should be replaced by some officer appointed directly by Her Majesty.

The events of the next few years placed Savory at the head of the colony. Millechamp returned to the Pacific, but took up his residence in Guam. Mazarra died, leaving a young widow, a pretty native of Guam. Savory married the widow, began to rear a family, and became the patriarchal magistrate. Cultivating his little farm, he sold to whalers the sweet potatoes which he raised and the rum which he distilled from sugar cane. He made considerable money, which he deposited in the ground; but one day he became too confidential and friendly with visitors from a schooner carrying the American flag, who carried away his money and his journal, taking with them also two women of his household, who afterwards declared, at Honolulu, they had no desire to return.

In 1853, Perry visited the settlement while on his expedition to Japan.[5] He found a population of thirty-one, of whom eight were whites, who had chosen good-natured wives from the Sandwich Islands emigrants. The people seemed happy and contented; they cultivated sweet potatoes, corn, pumpkins, onions, taro, watermelons, bananas and pineapples; they raised enough sugar and tobacco for their own consumption. Seeing the importance of the islands to commerce, between California and China, he made explorations, distributed seeds, left live stock and various

---

[5] Japan Expedition, vol. i, p. 201.

implements of husbandry, and purchased from Savory the title to a piece of land suitably located for the construction of buildings for a naval depot.[6]   In a report to the Secretary of the Navy, on June 25, he said if the Department desired he would take possession in the name of the United States. The inhabitants practically disowned the sovereignty of England, hoisting the British flag only as a signal on the arrival of a vessel. They recognized that they were able to take care of themselves and needed no foreign control.[7]

After Perry left, the settlers, following his suggestion and advice, met in convention at Savory's house and established a form of municipal government for the colony of Peel Island, electing Savory chief magistrate. The magistrate, acting with the two councilmen, who were also elected by the convention, were to serve for two years, and were given authority to make such rules and regulations as they should consider necessary for the public good. Such laws required the approval of two-thirds of the whole number of residents. Two pilots for the port were selected by unanimous vote and given authority to appoint capable substitutes. Among other regulations was one against the discharge of crews by captains when in the port. Another prohibited the enticing or secretion of deserters, placing the fine at $50. All penalties were to be pecuniary. The magistrate was to be the final court for all claims and disputes. He and the council were given power to direct the seizure and sale of any property of any offender, sufficient to liquidate fines against such offender. All fines were to constitute a public fund, kept by the chief magistrate and appropriated as he and the council might deem proper, but a published statement was to be made each year. At the end of each year, all unexpended moneys were to be equally divided, unless otherwise ordained by the convention. The

---

[6] Japan Expedition, vol. i, p. 211; vol. ii, pp. 127-33.
[7] Japan Expedition, vol. i, pp. 199-200.

magistrate and council were authorized, whenever they should consider it necessary, to call a convention of the people to amend or increase the laws.

In December, 1853, at Hong Kong, just before leaving for Japan, Perry was surprised to learn from Sir George Bonham, the English superintendent of trade, that his visit to the Bonins and his purchase of a coal depot had attracted the attention of Lord Clarendon, of the British Government, who, acting on a statement of Alexander Simpson, who had once been the British representative in the South Seas, gave instructions to ask some explanations.[8] In reply, while expressing his doubt of the right of Great Britain to claim sovereignty, Perry stated that the purchase of land was of a strictly private character, and without any instructions from Washington. The question of sovereignty he was willing to leave " to be discussed hereafter." [9]

---

[8] Japan Expedition, vol. i, p. 203.

[9] Perry favored colonies in those distant regions.

While at Maderia, en route to Japan to negotiate for commercial relations, safe harbors, and coaling stations, Perry (on Dec. 14, 1852,) wrote the Secretary of the Navy that as a preliminary step the United States should at once secure ports of refuge and supply on islands south of Japan, and conciliate the inhabitants so that our friendly purposes might be better understood by the Japanese Government. He suggested that the occupation of the principal ports of the Loo Choo Islands for the accommodation of warships and merchant vessels would be justified by the rules of moral law and necessity, and by the amelioration of the condition of the natives whom the Prince of Satsuma ruled by fear rather than by power to coerce obedience. Great Britain already held the most important points in the East India and Chinese seas. Perry, therefore, thought the United States should lose no time in adopting active measures to secure ports in the islands that fortunately were still left. [Sen. Exec. Doc. 34, 33-2, pp. 12-15.]

The President concurred in Perry's opinion, and Secretary Everett (Feb. 15, 1853) gave instructions to secure ports either in the Japanese islands or elsewhere, but to use no force except in the last resort. [Ibid., p. 15.] On Jan. 25, 1854, Perry, while at Napa in Great Loo Choo, wrote Secretary Dobbin of the navy that, in case of failure to negotiate with Japan, it was his aim " to take under the *surveillance* of the American flag, upon the ground of reclamation for insults and injuries committed upon American

Desiring to consummate an arrangement to fill up the remaining link of a great mail route of the world, he considered that the question of sovereignty was not so important as that of an open door for the hospitable reception of all nations.   At another time, speaking on the extension of American trade in the East, he said: " What benefits the commerce of the United States and extends American territory cannot but result advantageously to other powers." [10]

Perry's plan was to secure the organization of a stock company of merchants and artisans, to send two vessels laden with building materials and supplies for whalers and naval vessels, and as trade grew up, to send out young married people, gradually building up a thrifty community which would extend over the entire group and perhaps send missionaries to Japan, Formosa " and other benighted countries." [11]

Contemplating British rivalry in maritime enterprise, he had often suggested that commercial settlements in China and Pacific waters would be vitally necessary to the continued success of American commerce in those regions, but considered it unadvisable to erect for these settlements any defences except such as were necessary for protection against pirates and common marauders.[12]   After the success of his Japan expedition, speaking of the tendency to seek

---

citizens, this island of Great Loo Choo." The people seemed friendly, and he intimated that they should not be abandoned " as found, defenceless and overburdened." The President, however, feeling that such a course might prove embarassing, was " disinclined, without authority of Congress, to take and retain possession of an island in that distant country," unless demanded by more potent reasons. Secretary Dobbin wrote (May 23, 1854) in reply: " If, in future, resistance should be offered and threatened, it would also be rather mortifying to surrender the island, if once seized." He approved Perry's suggestions as to the establishment of a coal depot at Port Lloyd, however, and also his correspondence with Bonham, as to the sovereignty of the Bonins. [Sen. Exec. Doc. 34, 33-2, p. 112.]

[10] Japan Expedition, vol. ii, p. 180.
[11] Japan Expedition, vol. i, p. 212.
[12] Sen. Exec. Doc. 34, 33-2, Perry to Secy. of Navy, Dec. 14, 1852.

further expansion, he said: " Perhaps we cannot change the course of events, or avert our ultimate destiny. . . . It belongs to us to act honorably and justly . . . and to encourage changes in the political condition of Japan, China, and especially Formosa." He urged that in Formosa,[18] whose commanding position resembled that of Cuba, there should be an American commercial settlement from which communication might be established with China, Japan, Loo Choo, Cochin China, Cambodia, Siam and the Philippines. He quoted with approval the statement that colonies are as necessary to a commercial nation as ships and that it would be difficult for any government to prevent the establishment, in distant regions, of trading or religious settlements which would naturally grow into flourishing and self-governing communities.

The British consul at Yokohama, who visited Port Lloyd, in 1875, said Perry's code of government for the Bonins was never enforced, and soon forgotten. In the years following 1854, whalers and men-of-war visited the island occasionally, but the conditions were not favorable to rapid increase of population. In 1861, Japan made an effort to colonize Peel Island by sending 100 colonists from Yedo, but soon wearied of the scheme, and by 1863 all her settlers had withdrawn, leaving only a stone stating that the islands were discovered by Japan and were still her property.

By 1875 the community at Port Lloyd numbered 69— 37 male and 32 female, 20 being children, but only 5 were entirely white. The settlers, with their few wants supplied by whalers, still lived in rudely-constructed, sparsely-furnished cottages in sheltered nooks, cultivated patches of

---

[18] In Feb. 1857, Parker, the United States Commissioner in China suggested the policy of occupying Formosa. In his despatch to the Department of State he enclosed a letter from Gideon Nye, Jr., who urged occupation in the interest of humanity and commerce, and offered to assist in colonizing the island, if the United States would protect him. Sen. Exec. Doc. 22, 35-2, exhibit G., pp. 1203-04.

sugar cane and maize, raised pigs, geese and ducks, and caught turtle. They appeared to live in decency and order, and to be comfortable, but they had no thought of religion, and with the exception of one person, could not read or write. Life had often been insecure among them, eleven men having met violent deaths within twenty-five years. The settlers had a repugnance to settled government. Though the American flag was displayed from one of the huts, the American Government apparently had no idea of taking possession. By the opening of Japan to the world the Bonins became less important. They were left to the southward of the steamer line routes between the United States and the Orient, Yokohama being a more convenient and more desirable station. Mr. Robertson, the British consul at Yokohama, who visited Port Lloyd in 1875, proposed that Great Britain should take the Bonins beneath her sheltering wings, initiate some simple inexpensive form of government there, and attempt to guide the young settlement through its early perils.[14] Japan then seemed unable to colonize Yesso, right at her doors, but in 1878 she took undisputed possession of the whole Bonin group.

The United States, especially after the ratification of the treaty with Japan, probably had no desire to enter into discussion regarding questions of title to an island so far distant.[15] In 1835, Edmund Roberts, who had succeeded in negotiating a treaty with Siam, was instructed to endeavor studiously to inculcate upon all (including Japan) the idea that the United States, though strong and resourceful, had a history indicating no ambition for conquest and no desire for colonial possessions, and a policy whose essential part was to avoid political connection with any other government.[16]

Wilkes, during his explorations in 1841, had surveyed

---

[14] Chambers' Journal, July 5, 1879.
[15] See p. 52; also Senate Doc. 77, 20-2, February 16, 1829.
[16] 1 Sp. M. 131.

Wake Island (19 N. lat., 166 E. long.) and asserted title, but the United States Navy never took possession.[17] Webster, in June, 1852, agreed to send a naval vessel to protect American guano interests on the Lobos Islands which were not occupied by any of the South American States, and had been visited by American fishermen for half a century, but he decided to yield to the protests of Peru, who declared her ownership had never been questioned before.[18] Under an act of Congress of August 18, 1856, conferring discretionary power on the President to assume the ownership of guano islands discovered by United States citizens,[19] Commander Davis, of the *St. Mary's*, sailed from the coasts of Central America in 1858 and took formal possession of Jarvis and Nantucket islands in the name of the United States, and deposited in the earth a declaration to that effect. Lieutenant Brooke, in the next year, took possession of Bird and Necker islands, near the Hawaiian group.[20] In October, 1858, Cakobau, the principal chief of Bau, and also king of the whole Fiji group, in a document offering the sovereignty to Queen Victoria,[21] declared that his action was

---

[17] The United States took possession of Wake Island, in January, 1899, with a view to using it as a station on a cable-telegraph line between Hawaii and the Philippines.

[18] Sen. Exec. Rp. 109, 32-1, Aug. 21, 1852.

[19] Under this act the United States, in 1898, owned 57 islands and groups of islands in the Pacific, and 13 in the Caribbean sea.

[20] Report Secy. of Navy, Dec. 2, 1859.

[21] This deed of cession was ratified, and signed by 21 chiefs on December 14, 1859, and by others in August and September. The legislative assembly of New South Wales recommended the acceptance of the proffered sovereignty, and captains in the British navy recommended occupation, but after sending Dr. B. Seemann to secure further information, the British Government decided to decline the offer. Seemann reported that the islands would become a flourishing colony. American whaleships which had been getting supplies at Samoa or Tonga were now beginning to go to Fiji on account of the exorbitant prices recently asked by the natives of the former islands. [Berthold Seemann: Viti, Cambridge, Eng., 1862.] In 1864, an attempt was made to establish a regular government based on English models, but was not a success. Meanwhile the rumor went that the United States intended to

for the purpose of preventing severe measures threatened by the United States against the king and the sovereignty and the territory of the islands in case of the non-payment of a debt of $45,000 [22] which, under the existing state of affairs in the islands,[23] he would not be able to collect within the brief time stated in the contract.

In 1867, by the acquisition of Alaska, the United States became the owner of the Aleutian Islands, extending almost to the Asiatic coasts. On August 28 of the same year, Captain Reynolds, by order of the United States Navy, occupied the Midway Islands [28° 12′ north lat., 177° 22′ west long.] which had been discovered by Captain N. C. Brooks on July 5, 1859, and first occupied by the Pacific Mail Steamship Company in July, 1867.[24] The Senate Committee, in January, 1869, for both political and commercial reasons, favored making a naval station there, stating that the United States should have at least one harbor of refuge on the route to China, and should prevent the possibility of European occupation of any island which, under their control, might become another Nassau. The Secretary of the Navy, in his report of the previous December, had

---

assume the protectorate. In 1869, Lord Granville considered that there would be "more disadvantage in Great Britain taking the responsibility of the government of Fiji than in the risk of the United States assuming the Protectorate." [Parl. Papers, 1875.] But the Australian colonies at the Conference of 1870 called for British annexation, and Lord Kimberly decided to send a commission to report. The report of Commander Goodenough and Mr. Layard was strongly in favor of annexation. The cession was accepted in October, 1874, and the islands were organized as a crown colony with Sir Arthur Gordon as Governor.
[Egerton: History of English Colonial Policy, p. 396.]

[22] Quarterly Review, July, 1859, p. 203.

[23] The Fijis, which had become the resort of the European trader, "threatened to become an anarchic Hell." [Egerton: History of English Colonial Policy, p. 396.]
The natives, however, were not such ferocious cannibals as they had formerly been. [Quarterly Review, July, 1859, p. 203.]

[24] Senate Rp. 194, 40-3, Jan. 28, 1869. Sen. Exec. Doc. 79, 40-2. Report of Secy. of the Navy, 1870, p. 8, and 1871, pp. 6, 7 and 8.

said the rapid increase of Pacific commerce and of American interests springing up in connection with our recent extensive acquisitions, our rising States on the Pacific, ever-increasing intimacy with the islands of the ocean, made the United States interested beyond any other power in giving security to mariners in the Pacific. On March 1, 1869, the sum of $50,000 was appropriated for opening a harbor at Midway; but, after spending that amount, it was seen that $400,000 would be required, and the plan was abandoned. The United States, however, still owns the island.

CHAPTER VII.

UNLOCKING THE GATES OF THE ORIENT.

Until a comparatively recent date, the Orient remained a sealed mystery to the nations of Western civilization and progress.[1] It was only by the persistent and increasingly determined efforts of foreigners that Japan was finally induced to open her doors and windows. China, assuming an arrogant supremacy, though she had permitted a limited trade, endeavored to erect barriers of exclusiveness, but was finally forced to be more liberal in commercial relations, and slowly extended her intercourse with the younger and more progressive nations of the West.

Japan.—The Japanese policy from 1637[2] to 1854 was one of exclusion and inclusion—to keep the world out and the Japanese at home—and the Dutch factory at Deshema of Nagasaki was the only window or loophole of observation during that time. All attempts by foreigners to secure trading advantages were successfully resisted. The strict isolation of Japan, closing her eyes to keep out the light of the universe, and refusing to open her arms to the West,

---

[1] Humboldt once said that the narrow neck of land forming the isthmus of Panama had been the "bulwark of the independence of China and Japan."

[2] Between 1542 and 1600 Christian missionaries exerted considerable influence in Japan. By 1581 there were 200 churches and 150,000 converts. A few years later the rivalry of the opposing orders, the Spanish Jesuits and the Portuguese Franciscans, created animosities, and resulted in persecution by the Japanese. At the battle of Sekigahara, in 1600, in which 10,000 lives were lost, the Christian army (of Southern Japan) was defeated. A reactionary policy of the conservatives followed, and an edict of 1606 prohibited Christianity. The last Christian uprising was defeated in 1636.

provoked American enterprise which elsewhere had been mastering opposition. As early as 1815 Commodore Porter proposed an expedition to open trade, and Monroe intended to send him, but the plans were never matured.[3]

In 1832 (as previously stated), just after the plunder of the American ship *Friendship* at Quallah Battoo, Captain Edmund Roberts,[4] who had been well acquainted with the commerce of the Far East, was sent as United States confidential agent to negotiate for treaties.[5] He was instructed to proceed to Japan to open trade, in case he found prospects favorable, but he was directed not to enter the country until he should receive assurance that nothing unbecoming the dignity of the United States would be required. Though he succeeded in securing a treaty with Siam[6] and the Sultan

---

[3] De Bow's, Dec., 1852. In 1797, the *Eliza* of New York, carrying the American flag with seventeen stars, sailed to Nagasaki, under the command of Capt. Steward, but did not open trade. Capt. John Derby, of Salem, Mass., soon made an unsuccessful attempt to open trade. In 1803, Capt. Steward returned to Nagasaki, but found that the Japanese desired no American products except ginseng. The discovery of valuable whale fisheries near the Kurile Islands, and southward, increased the importance of friendly relations with Japan. Soon there began a long story of shipwrecked seamen who were imprisoned by the Japanese. J. Q. Adams denied the right of Japan to remain a hermit nation, but his was "the voice of one crying in the wilderness."

[4] See pp. 48 and 68.

[5] Sen. Exec. Doc. 34, 33-2, Jan. 31, 1855. Sen. Exec. Doc. 59, 32-1, vol. ix, Apr. 8, 1852.

[6] In Siam, with her old and venerable code of crude and incomplete laws, where the creditor still had absolute power over the life and property of the debtor, American commerce had been subject to any pecuniary extortions or other impositions which avarice might inflict. At Bankok, on March 30, 1833, Roberts, secured a treaty of amity and commerce, nine feet and seven inches long, removing the imposition on imports, releasing debtors from pains and penalties in case they delivered all their property, fixing port charges, allowing American citizens to trade directly with private individuals instead of through the king who had hitherto fixed prices and delayed trade, and obviating the necessity of enormous presents to officials. [Edmund Roberts: Embassy to the Eastern Courts of Cochin China, Siam and Muscat in the Sloop *Peacock*, 1832-34. N. Y., 1837.] A new treaty was

of Muscat, and began negotiations with Cochin China, he
did not proceed to Borneo [7] nor to Japan.

In 1837 C. W. King, a merchant, went to Japan in the
unarmed *Morrison* to return some shipwrecked Japanese,
who had been saved from a junk which had gone ashore
near the mouth of the Columbia river in 1831, but his vessel being fired upon at Yedo, he returned without succeed-
ing in his mission.[8] The Japanese probably understood
that his principal motive was to open commercial intercourse. In 1845 the *Manhattan*, of Sag Harbor, attempting
to return several castaways, met with a similar reception.
In the same year Zadoc Pratt, of New York, laid before the
House a report advising hostility and proposing to send an
embassy to Japan and Corea.

The successful negotiation of a treaty with China in 1844
increased the efforts to secure communication with Japan.
In 1846 Commodore Biddle, by instructions of May 22,

---

negotiated by Mr. Harris in May, 1856, and was ratified by the
United States the next year. It was modified in 1867. Relations
with Siam have remained undisturbed, the United States enjoying
the rights and immunities extended to the most favored nation.
In 1884 an agreement regulating the liquor traffic in Siam was
concluded.

Roberts had also endeavored to secure a treaty with Cochin
China, but after engaging in a protracted correspondence and
enduring much Eastern prevarication he failed on account of disagreement as to conventionalities and excessive formalities. But
he made a treaty with the Sultan of Muscat, who wrote Andrew
Jackson an extravagantly figurative and loving letter. After the
Siam treaty had been ratified by the United States Senate in June,
1834, Roberts was sent to exchange ratifications, and renewed
negotiations with Cochin China, whose etiquette as to titles he
met by a ruse diplomatique, but whose consent to a treaty he was
unable to obtain. [W. S. Ruschenberger: A Voyage Around the
World, including an Embassy to Muscat and Siam, 1836-37.
Phila., 1838.] He died at Macao, June 12, 1836.

[7] On June 23, 1850, at Bruni, Joseph Balestier concluded with the
Sultan of Borneo a convention of amity, commerce and navigation,
securing liberty of residence and trade, protection of United States
citizens and shipwrecked seamen, the privilege of extraditionality,
and the use of ports for war vessels.

[8] Perry: U. S. Japan Expedition, vol. i, pp. 47-49.

1845, sailed to Yedo bay and remained ten days, but failed in his peaceful attempt to gain access to the country. He was informed that, by law, no trade could be allowed with any foreign nation except Holland, and that every nation had a right to manage its own affairs in its own way. He received an anonymous, undated communication asking him to depart as soon as possible and to consult his own safety by not appearing again upon the coast. While on board a Japanese junk to receive the official reply, he also received an unpleasant push from a common Japanese soldier. Captain Glynn afterwards (1851) said that Biddle was too lenient.

A. H. Everett, of the United States legation at Macao, who had received full power to negotiate with the Japanese Government, but had transferred it to Biddle, and who still had power to renew the attempt at a treaty in case any new combination of circumstances should increase the prospect of success, wrote Secretary Buchanan on January 5, 1847, that perhaps Biddle's attempt to open negotiations had not been made with sufficient discretion, and had " placed the subject in a rather less favorable position than it stood before."

Americans, following the whale to the far off seas, were sometimes wrecked on the coast of the Kurile Islands, and arrested and cast into Japanese prisons. Even while Biddle was at Yedo bay, though the Japanese did not mention it, it seems that American citizens (from the *Lawrence*, which had been wrecked May 27, 1846) were already in Japanese prisons. After repeated " trials " they were released through the kindness of the Dutch director at Nagasaki. Other sailors from American vessels, having been thrown upon the coasts of Japan in 1848, were imprisoned as spies,[9] and some were punished for attempting to escape, or for other insubordination.

---

[9] On April 14, 1847, the Netherlands' *chargé d'affaires* notified Buchanan that Japan, in 1843 had given warning against the exploration of Japanese coasts.

With the settlement of the Oregon question and the acquisition of California, and a corresponding expansion of opportunity and duty, the United States became more vigilant in guarding American interests in the Pacific, and more determined to break down Oriental exclusiveness. On January 31, 1849, Commander Geisinger, of the United States East India squadron, hearing in Chinese waters that sixteen Americans were imprisoned, sent Commander Glynn with the United States ship *Preble*[10] to demand their release.[11] The Japanese officials first threatened offensive operations, then assumed haughty indifference, and finally tried evasive diplomacy, but they acceded to Glynn's peremptory demand for the immediate delivery of the prisoners.[12]

Glynn, on returning to New York, was enthusiastic in his desire to secure some arrangement which would divert the commerce of half the human family from foreign channels into the bosom of the United States. On February 24, 1851, he wrote Howland and Aspinwall that he had found a strong interest on both sides of the Pacific in favor of establishing a line of steamers between Asia and America; and he suggested that Shanghai should be the terminus, and that an effort should be made to secure coal from Formosa and Japan.[13] He proposed that the United States desiring fuel and depots in Japan, and having good cause for quarrel, should go on with the recent congressional inquiry into the Japanese imprisonment of Americans, ask redress, and compel them to adjust the controversy by

---

[10] The *Preble* had sailed from New York in September, 1846, during the Mexican war. She was at Honolulu during the trouble of the French with the Hawaiian Government in November, 1849. Later, at San Francisco, many of her crew were discharged, and others ran for the " gold diggings." She arrived at New York January 2, 1851. [N. Y. Herald, Jan. 3, 1851. In Sen. Exec. Doc. 59, 32-1, Apr. 8, 1852.]
[11] H. Exec. Doc. 84, 31-1, vol. x, Aug. 15, 1850.
[12] Perry: U. S. Japan Expedition, vol. i.
[13] Sen. Exec. Doc. 59, 32-1, vol. 9, p. 59.

granting depot privileges in some Japanese port. Reflecting on the possible necessity of using force, he said: "We could convert their selfish government into a liberal republic in a short time; such an unnatural system would, at the present day, fall to pieces upon the slightest concussion. But it is better to go to work peaceably with them if we can. . . . If I read the signs aright this is the time for action."

On June 10, 1851, Glynn, urging that intercourse with Japan was demanded by the interests of civilization, and should be secured, by peaceable means if possible, or by force if necessary, advised the President to select some naval officers of tact,[14] able to conduct hostile operations if necessary, to bear to the Japanese Government a document that would be a future justification before the world, disclaiming any desire to interfere with internal affairs, and making no complaints for past conduct. He suggested that the Dutch should be conciliated, and that England, who was alarmed at our strides in the East, should be reconciled by the assurance that we were asking Japan for no exclusive privileges.

President Fillmore had already decided, in the interests of commerce and humanity, to send an envoy to make another appeal to Japan for friendly intercourse, and to endeavor to secure coaling facilities for the line of steamers projected by American citizens. On May 10, 1851, he wrote a letter to the emperor, informing him that the United States had expanded to the Pacific; that in order to form the last link in the chain of navigation, American ships must pass near Japanese shores; and that we desired trade, and needed the coal which Providence had deposited in Japan for the human family.

Commodore Aulick, in command of the East Indian naval

---

[14] Glynn said Biddle's visit of 1846, was unfavorable to the United States—the Japanese and Loo Choo Islanders having given out exaggerated reports of his chastisement.

forces, was instructed by Webster, on June 10, 1851, as a special (non-missionary) envoy to make an effort to secure from the Japanese the assurance of supplies of coal at fair prices, either in Japanese ports or on some near island easy of access, the right of access for American trading vessels, and the promise of protection of shipwrecked sailors and property.   In 1852, his powers were transferred to Commodore Perry.

On November 13, 1852, Commodore M. C. Perry,[15] invested with both naval and diplomatic power, was instructed to go to Japan with an imposing fleet (as a manifestation of power) to state that we sought no interference with religion and we were connected with no European government, and to use all amicable means to secure a treaty of friendship and commerce, but to resort to no force unless in self-defence in protecting his vessels or crews, or to resent acts of personal violence to himself or officers.   He was directed to show that our forbearance had not resulted from timidity; and, in case argument failed to secure a treaty, he was to change his tone and inform Japan that American citizens, driven to her coasts by wind and weather, must be treated with humanity.   He was to use caution and vigilance, and all journals and private notes of persons in the expedition were considered to be United States property until the Navy Department should give permission to publish them.[16]

The letter which he carried from President Fillmore to the Japanese emperor, urged the necessity of new laws, from time to time, to meet such new conditions of the world as those resulting from American expansion to the Pacific,

---

[15] M. C. Perry (1794-1858) had served as a boy in the War of 1812, and against the pirates in the West Indies, and in the capture of Vera Cruz (1847) and belonged to the same combative stock as O. H. Perry, the author of that laconic dispatch: "We have met the enemy and they are ours."   His idea was to occupy one of the Loo Choo Islands as a stronghold from which to terrorize Japan, but Fillmore counselled peace.

[16] Sen. Exec. Doc. 34, 33-2, Jan. 31, 1855.

the sudden growth of California, whose trade with the East was rapidly increasing, and the development of steam navigation which required coal depots. " There was a time," said the President, " when the ancient laws of your Imperial Majesty's government were first made." It was suggested that the experiment of trade might at least be tried for five years.

Several persons, including von Siebold, a German, who had been banished from Japan, and was supposed to be employed as a Russian spy, made application to join the expedition in the interests of science, but their applications were refused in the interests of order.

On November 24, with models of American inventions and other articles for presents, Perry sailed from Norfolk via Cape of Good Hope, and on May 4, 1853, he reached Shanghai.

He resolved to act with firmness and decision, and to refuse to meet any but an officer of the highest rank.

At Napa, of the Loo Choo Islands, where he stopped to get provisions and to make explorations, he declined to receive two dignitaries who came alongside his vessel to present their enormous red cards. By the advice of the English missionary, he asked an immediate conference with the chief authority of the islands. On May 28, the regent, with a score of attendants, actively fluttering their fans to reduce their temperature, were received on board the *Susquehanna* with great ceremony and granted the requests to sell provisions, permit surveys, and allow the officers a house on shore. When the officers visited the shore, most of the merchants closed their shops, and the gentry turned upon their heels and disappeared. For the provisions which the natives carried to the ship the officials received the profits. Some of Perry's men, accompanied by Loo Choo spies, whom they walked almost out of breath, explored nearly one-half the island in six days, but they had no opportunity to converse with the people or to see their interior life.

Perry resolved to pay a return visit to the regent in the palace of Sheudi. The regent sent a long diplomatic roll, stating that the " Queen Dowager " had been ill since the visit of the British admiral, who invaded the sacred palace. Perry, expressing deep sorrow, offered to send one of his surgeons to her. Seated in a sedan chair, carried by four " coolies," and accompanied by a gay procession of 200 persons, he went to the palace of the capital. He was met with profound salutations by a throng of officials with flowing robes, fans and umbrellas, and was ushered into the " elevated enclosure [hall] of fragrant festivities " where the Americans received weak tea, " dabs of gingerbread," and tobacco. Then he accompanied the regent into his own private residence where, with chopsticks, they partook of a twelve-course Loo Choo dinner, and drank to the health of the Queen Dowager and son and to the prosperity of the people.

After a brief visit to the Bonin Islands, where he took possession of the Bailey or Coffin group in the name of the United States, and purchased land for a coal depot at Port Lloyd, Perry returned to Loo Choo on June 23 and was surprised to find that the regent, though still in full possession of his faculties, had been deposed and replaced by a younger man. After astonishing the people by exhibitions of the Daguerrotype, telegraph, submarine armor, etc., he sailed away (July 2), feeling that they would be glad to see him return, and that it was his duty to protect them as far as possible against the " vindictiveness of their cruel rulers," who favored exclusiveness.

Sailing to Japan, Perry entered the bay below Yedo on July 8, where his presence, and his refusal to heed the scrolls of warning which minor officials held out before him, created considerable excitement. He refused to go to Nagasaki, insisted upon talking with none but the highest dignitary, and his persistence finally induced the Governor of Urago to apply to the shogun, who, being embarrassed both from without and within, arranged for an official conference on July 14, at which two venerable princes received President Fillmore's letter and presents. Notwithstanding Japanese intimations that it was now time to go, he resolved to go farther up the bay. It seemed that the nearer he approached the imperial city the more polite and friendly the officials became. When he informed Yezaimon and Tatsnoski of his intention to leave on July 17, the latter expressed regret, endeavored to drown their grief in fresh supplies of wine, grew very affectionate, and whispered that all would be well with the President's letter.

Sailing to Hong Kong, Perry refitted his vessels, giving the Japanese time to come to a decision. His return was hastened by the suspicious movements of French and Russian vessels in Eastern seas. He feared that there might be an attempt to forestall the American negotiations, or to obtain a foothold in Japan by lending aid to the latter in case of collision with the Americans. On February 13, passing the Japanese boats, he confidently advanced up Yedo bay to the " American anchorage," where he proposed to meet the Japanese officials. After ten days' "negotiation" he moved near enough to Yedo to hear the striking of the night watches, and obtained the promise of a conference at Yokohama. In a specially prepared "Treaty House," on March 8, 1854, he met five Japanese officials who, with imposing ceremonies, submitted a long roll containing a reply to the President's letter. The shogun had sent copies of the letter to most of the daimios and had received from many of them answers adverse to the opening of the country, but, after prolonged conferences he consented to a favorable treaty which was completed on March 31, and conceded the opening of Shimoda and Hakodate to American vessels. His power was already tottering, and Japan would have been revolutionized from within if she had not been invaded from without.

Perry's treaty far exceeded expectations, and other powers were not slow in securing the advantages which he had gained. A Russian admiral had stopped at Nagasaki in the

6

latter part of 1853 and demanded a neighborly attitude, the opening of ports, and a settlement of the boundaries of Sagalien.   On November 12 he had made a proposition to join forces and cooperate with the Americans, but Perry civilly declined to take any step which might be interpreted as " inconsistent with our policy of abstaining from all alliance with foreign powers." [17]   Perhaps a Japanese distrust of the purposes of Russia had some influence in causing the success of the American negotiations.   The Dutch, who in 1852, had advised Japan to change its policy of exclusion in favor of all peaceful nations, claimed that they had aided in securing Perry's success, but Perry had never invoked their aid and was not willing to admit their claim.

Having made a good beginning, the United States, in the interests of trade and international relations, and, with a spirit of tolerance, liberality and justice toward Japan, sought new concessions.   In 1857 Townsend Harris, who had been residing at Shimoda as United States consul-general, negotiated a treaty enlarging the privileges granted in 1854 and securing the opening of the port of Nagasaki and the right of permanent residence for Americans at the ports of Shimoda and Hakodate.   At Yedo, in 1858, without any show of force or compulsion, he won a diplomatic triumph which revolutionized the relations of Japan with the world. By firm, honest diplomacy he concluded with the shogun's ministers a treaty providing for unrestricted commercial relations, diplomatic representation at Yedo, rights of residence, trade at certain ports, regulation of duties, religious freedom and extra-territoriality.[18]

Other powers soon concluded similar treaties.   It was agreed that the President, at the request of Japan, would act as mediator between the latter and European powers with whom she might have questions of dispute.

Unfortunately, under the new commercial policy, prices

---

[17] Perry: U. S. Japan Expedition, vol. i, p. 61.
[18] Sen. Exec. Doc. 25, 36-1.

in Japan rose from 100 per cent to 300 per cent. Soon after the beginning of the American war, cotton rose to over 30 cents per pound. The *samaurai,* or military class, who suffered most, encouraged the idea that hatred of foreigners was loyalty to Japan. In 1862 the mikado ordered the "barbarians" to be expelled, and summoned the shogun to Kioto to give an account of his stewardship. The shogun, who saw his power declining, and the daimios deserting him to flock to Kioto, was induced through pressure to proclaim to foreign nations that the ports of Japan were to be closed against foreign intercourse. The foreigners now learned that the shogun was not the real emperor, but they were firm in the purpose to let slip no advantage already gained.

In Japan, as in China, Secretary Seward, who desired to substitute fair diplomacy for force, insisted upon the policy of cooperation of the powers, based on community of interests. He was opposed to intervention in internal affairs, but when the daimio of Nagato, opposing the shogun's treaties, closed the strait of Shimonoseki and fired on an American merchant steamer, the naval forces of the United States, Great Britain, France and the Netherlands, with the approval of the shogun's government, and in order to enforce treaty rights, opened the strait by force, and compelled the surrender of the hostile daimio.[19] He favored a policy of neutrality with reference to internal struggles, but desired the establishment and maintenance of a strong central government by which treaties might be enforced, and native autonomy preserved.

The bombardment by the powers, together with the report of a Japanese embassy which returned from Europe in 1864, had a profound effect on the Japanese mind, and the emperor, with whom the powers began to direct nego-

---

[19] Out of a total indemnity fund of $3,000,000 to the combined powers, the United States received $785,000 which was afterwards returned (1883).

tiations from Hiago below Kioto in 1865, yielded to ratification of treaties in spite of popular prejudice. The daimios who had at first opposed the shogun's policy, now acquiesced in the new policy of the mikado, who was soon restored to his ancient power, and encouraged the adoption of Western civilization.

In 1866, England, France, Holland and the United States agreed to a convention practically depriving Japan of the right to regulate its tariff beyond five per cent on imports and exports.[20] Though in 1872 Japan failed in her negotiations for a revision of treaties, the United States, since the growth of the imperial authority in Japan,[21] has been willing to release the latter from the treaty limitations upon its judicial and fiscal independence.[22]

China.—In 1784 the Stars and Stripes, floating from the *Empress of China*, an American trading vessel, first appeared in the Orient at Canton, the only Chinese port at which foreigners were permitted to trade. In 1786, President Washington, in the interests of a rapidly growing trade, appointed Samuel Shaw as consul at that port. It was over a half-century later that China first consented to make treaties regulating and extending commercial intercourse, and providing for the protection of the lives and property of American citizens on Chinese territory. From 1786 to 1844 the American consuls at Canton were merely merchants. During that time, however, our trade with China suffered only one temporary interruption—in 1821, when Terranora, a sailor on board of the American ship *Emily*, was judicially murdered by the Chinese magistrate, Pwanyu,

---

[20] Treaties and Conventions, 1889, p. 612.

[21] See an article by Matsuyama Makato in vol. cxxvii of N. Am. Review, pp. 406-26. On the civil discord which resulted in Japanese reforms, see Sen. Exec. Doc. 65, 40-2, vol. ii, May 23, 1868.

[22] See the Commercial Convention of 1878, and the Treaty of Commerce and Navigation of November 22, 1894, which went into effect July 17, 1899.

and the American merchants at Whampoa protested without effect.[23]

For many years the powers of Western Europe had been able to secure a restricted trade.[24] As early as 1537 the Portuguese temporarily established a trade at Macao. They were soon followed by the Spanish, who had established a colony at Manila in 1543. In 1622 the Dutch attacked the Portuguese settlements at Macao and occupied the Pescadore (Pang-hu) Islands, and in 1625 they were induced to move to Formosa by Chinese promises of freedom of trade, but were driven to Java, a generation later, by the fleet of Koshinga, the pirate. In 1637 Captain Weddel, with an English squadron, anchored off Macao and compelled the opening of trade with the English. Soon after 1689 Russian caravans were premitted to go to Peking to trade. All attempts to secure commercial treaties or regular diplomatic intercourse, however, had ended in failure. Most ambassadors refused to make the nine prostrations required by the emperor as a preliminary to negotiation. In 1699 the English East India Company obtained permission to establish a factory and a consulate at Canton, where they desired to trade in tea, but trade was often interrupted by heavy duties and extortions. The Dutch finally secured the same privilege. No other port was open to commerce.

For half a century after 1720 all business of Europeans was transacted through a single company of Chinese hong merchants, which was responsible to the Chinese Government for the customs and duties, and responsible to no one for its enormous profits. Though the co-hong was dissolved in 1771, the hong merchants, by making presents to

---

[23] 14 De Bow, Apr., 1853, p. 359. Terranora accidentally killed a Chinese woman by dropping a pot on her head. He was finally given up to the Chinese authorities, who strangled him outside of the walls. [G. F. Train: An American Merchant in Europe, Asia and Australia. N. Y. 1847.]

[24] Early relations of the Western Powers with China are fully treated in R. Montgomery Martin's " China, Political, Commercial and Social." [Official Report, London, 1847, 2 vols.]

the Canton magistrates, still contrived to maintain their monopoly and continued their exorbitant and extortionate prices, and in some cases refused to pay their debts. Suspecting that their complaints were never allowed to reach Peking, the British, in 1792, sent to the imperial city an ambassador (Lord Macartney), who secured the dismissal of the Canton viceroy who had encouraged the frauds. In 1816, they again complained of the manner of the Canton trade and asked for new ports more convenient to the principal tea district, but Lord Amherst, who was sent at the head of an embassy, was not received by the Chinese sovereign.

After the expiration (1833) of the charter of the East India Company, which had traded as a supplicant to whom the Chinese granted favors, the Western world began its demand for the admission to China of individual merchants who desired to trade. In July, 1834, Lord Napier, with instructions from Lord Palmerston, arrived at Canton and demanded trade as a right. The Chinese refused to enter into any kind of negotiations to trade with " barbarians." After a period of irritation growing out of opium smuggling, they precipitated war by issuing a decree suspending all trade with England, who, in turn, resolved to bombard the exclusive Asiatics and oblige them to open the country to foreigners who desired to walk civilly through it. Unable to cope with British gunpowder, they soon began to receive fresh light from new lamps. In the peace negotiations of 1842, at the close of the so-called " Opium War," they agreed to pay the expenses of the war, cede Hong Kong to Great Britain and open five ports, including that of Fuchau, which the British had especially desired. The commercial privileges which England secured by the cannon's mouth were soon granted to other nations who sought them.

The United States was not slow to take advantage of the Chinese reformed methods of intercourse. In September, 1839, when the Chinese suspected that Americans were cooperating with the British, P. W. Snow, the American consul at Canton, had declined to conform to the troublesome Chinese literary conventionalities which the author-ities asked him to insert in his reply to the edicts of the imperial commissioner.[25] In December, 1842, President Tyler sent to the Senate and the House a message,[26] prepared by Webster,[27] referring to the importance of the Sandwich Islands and the China trade,[28] and urging an appropriation for sending an official representative to China. A bill for a mission was called up by the Senate at midnight on the last day of the session of 1842-43. It met with much opposition. Benton, on the ground that we already had trade and could never have closer relations than that with a people so distant and peculiar, said there was no necessity for a treaty. The appropriation was voted, however, and Edward Everett was selected (March 3) as the first envoy.[29] When the latter declined, Caleb Cushing was appointed. His instructions,[30] signed by Webster, were designed to dispel the Chinese delusion that other nations were dependents, and their representatives tribute bearers. He was directed to announce to the Chinese that the United States " pays tribute to none and expects tribute from none," but desires friendship and the protection of rights.

Arriving at Macao in the *Brandywine* in February, 1844, he soon opened correspondence with the authorities near Canton, who kept him in diplomatic contention until the middle of May. Failing to induce the Oriental mind to allow him to go to Peking, he was finally persuaded to abandon that part of his plan. Pen and ink prevailed over thoughts of cannon and ammunition. On the arrival of

---

[25] H. Exec. Doc. 119, 26-1, Feb. 21, 1840, 85 pp.

[26] Richardson's Messages, p. 211.

[27] Curtis's Webster, p. 176.

[28] In 1841 the imports of the United States from China were valued at $9,000,000, and her direct exports to China were $715,000 for domestic goods and $485,000 foreign goods.

[29] 5 Stat. at Large, p. 624.

[30] Sen. Exec. Doc. 138, 28-2, Feb. 21, 1845, 9 pp.

an imperial commissioner, Cushing decided that it was best "to dispose of all the commercial questions by treaty before venturing on Peking," where the Chinese ceremonial required ambassadors to undergo a series of prostrations and bumping of the head on the ground before the footstool of the Chinese " Son of Heaven." [31]   On July 3, at Wang Hiya, near Macao, he concluded with Keying [32] a treaty of peace, amity and commerce, opening the five ports to American commerce, establishing port regulations, allowing American citizens the privileges of residence, cemeteries and hospitals, conceding the right of foreigners to be tried before their consuls; granting to the United States the privilege of direct correspondence with the Imperial Government (to be transmitted by designated port officers), and promising all the privileges and advantages which China might grant to other nations. [33]

The United States, by her peaceful but firm policy, with no desire for Chinese territory, secured greater prestige and concession than the British.

In 1845 Cushing returned to the United States via the west coast of Mexico and Vera Cruz.   At that time, he, like many others, probably did not foresee the swiftly-coming events which a few years later contributed to the necessity of revising the treaty and enforcing its provisions more rigidly.   There were then no railways to the Pacific.   California was not yet an Anglo-Saxon community.   Uninspired prophecy declared that the Pacific coast would never be a part of the territory under the control of the United States Government.   In less than three years thereafter, we had expanded to the Pacific, a line of American steamers were nearly ready to run from Panama to California and Oregon, and we were preparing to shorten the distance to

---

[31] Benton: Thirty Years' View, vol. ii. H. Doc. 69, 28-2, vol. ii, Jan. 22, 1845, 14 pp.

[32] Keying appeared to be a man of relatively liberal views. He was unfortunate in his subsequent career.

[33] H. Doc. 69, 28-2, vol. ii, Jan. 22, 1845, 14 pp.

the Far East, and increase intercourse, by a transcontinental railway, and a regular, swift line of steamers between California and China [34] via the Sandwich Islands.

After Commodore Biddle had exchanged the ratified Cushing treaty, Alexander H. Everett was sent as our representative at Canton; but he soon died and was succeeded by John W. Davis, who managed to obtain an interview with the Imperial Commissioner at Canton, in 1848, and organized our peculiar judicial system in China.[35]

In his message of December, 1851, President Fillmore announced that the office of Commissioner to China remained unfilled—that several persons, to whom the place had been offered, had declined because of the inadequacy

---

[34] H. Rp. 596, 30-1, vol. iii, May 4, 1848.   37 pp.
American interests in the Pacific and the Far East had "attained great magnitudes." In January, 1846, there were 736 American ships (233,149 tons), and 19,560 officers and seamen engaged in the whale fisheries. Their annual product was about $10,000,000, and they spent about $3,000,000 in foreign ports, annually, for refreshments and repairs. Besides the whaling industry, we also had 200 vessels (75,000 tons) and 5000 seamen engaged in the Pacific carrying trade—exclusive of the commerce with China. These considerations, induced the House committee on naval affairs to urge the necessity of a naval depot on the California coast, as a part of the proposed plans for facilitating intercourse between the Mississippi river and China. The committee said: "Our commerce with China possesses the elements of indefinite expansion." Under the new Chinese policy, which had released trade from the vexatious monopolistic control of extortionate, capricious mandarins, Chinese imports from foreign countries had increased from $10,-205,370 in 1842 to $17,843,249 in 1844, and her exports from $13,-339,750, in 1842 to $25,513,370 in 1844, exclusive of the opium trade.
By 1852, the American trade with China amounted to $18,000,000 annually; but since the beginning of our trade with China, our imports had exceeded our exports more than $180,000,000, which had been paid in silver. John P. Kennedy, Secretary of the Navy, suggested that China might be induced to receive American tobacco as a substitute for poisonous opium. [Sen. Exec. Doc. 49, 32-2, Feb. 16, 1853.]
[35] See Sen. Exec. Doc. 72, 31-1, Sept. 9, 1850. (Davis' report as to consular courts.)
Mr. Davis was not able to find an American lawyer in all China, Hong Kong, Macao, or the Philippine Islands.

of the salary of $6,000 to meet the expense of living. A year later he appointed Humphrey Marshall, who accepted, and arrived in China at the beginning of 1853, with a letter to the emperor, and instructions to seek more satisfactory regulation of intercourse. [See Appendix.]

The vast changes in conditions since the United States had stood alone in the solitude of her first territorial limits, brought new duties and greater opportunities. Then the possession of Florida and Louisiana by European powers was a source of anxiety to the fathers of the republic. Now, we had annexed the neighbors whom we had formerly feared. Then the trans-Mississippi and the trans-Rocky territories were open to the conquest of foreigners. Now, the Pacific alone intervened between us and Asia, and Europe looked with amazement and admiration upon the giant strides of the youthful but vigorous republic. While we had been advancing by expansion, the wonders of science had brought us into closer proximity with all of the powers of the world. In our weak beginning, when we were embarrassed by the wars of Europe, Washington gave a warning against foreign entanglements, which became stereotyped into a political proverb, but now people began to ask: " Can the country continue to regard itself apart from Europe and the world? " " Would not the new conditions require the United States to be a part of any great political transaction which affects the history of the world? " We were interested especially in the relations and policies of the great colonizing nations of Europe. Feeling that relations with the East would constitute the most important factor in the achievements of the future, some went so far as to advocate an Anglo-American alliance [36] to preserve the

---

[36] W. H. Trescot, whose name figured later in the foreign relations of the United States, in 1849, stating that the Russian colonial system must be an exclusive one, and believing that the recent British economic policy indicated that Great Britain was " willing to share with the United States the divided allegiance of the world " considered that an alliance should be a part of our foreign

integrity of China and an open door, and to arrest the increasing power and growing antagonism of England and Russia in the direction of Asia, which was now our near neighbor.   The United States, therefore, felt as much concern in the affairs of the East as any nation in Europe.

The year which Marshall spent in China was one of great political confusion.   Revolution sought to remedy the chronic diseases of the empire.   Part of the political organism undertook to throw off superincumbent weight which had been sustained for years.[37].   Taiping[38] affairs culminated,

---

policy.   He considered it the only means to frustrate Russian designs, and, at the same time, preserve the independence of China. Spain was too feeble to interfere, and Austria and Prussia were only " accidents and convenient outworks of other nations." France, who (excepting England) was the only European power possessing a basis for independent action was still the natural ally of Russia, as she was at Tilsit.   " Equally as natural," said Trescot, " and equally as necessary, is the alliance between England and the United States. . . . The future history of the world must be achieved in the East. . . . The United States and Great Britain by concerted action on the ocean can control the history of the world. . . . Indeed, how can it be otherwise.   We are the two great commercial nations of modern history, . . . with the same language and ancestry. . . . And while the interest, both of England and the United States, lies in the monopoly of their Asiatic trade, each Government is peculiarly adapted for its respective part in the accomplishment of so important an end. . . . Thus allied in an honest unity of interest, the United States becomes England's strength, against the world, in support of her Indian colonies, and, shut out from territorial aggrandizement themselves, the United States, are thus by alliance with England—sharers of a common basis for further operations."

[37] See an article in 15 De Bow, Dec. 1853, pp. 541-71:   China and the Indies—Our " Manifest Destiny " in the East.

[38] The religious movement which developed into the Taiping rebellion was organized in the interior of China by Hung Sew-tsuen, a schoolmaster, who had been influenced by Christian books and had renounced Buddhism.   His followers resisted exactions, were persecuted, and finally arming themselves for self-defence, destroyed temples, and in October, 1850, won an important victory over the imperial soldiery.   Moving northward, they conquered as they went.   In March, 1853, they captured Nanking, which became Hung's capital in 1860.   In 1853, they also took Shanghai.   Their success thrilled the world, but political corruption and fanaticism

and the fate of the imperial dynasty was hanging in the balance. The imperial officials were too busy to attend to foreign affairs. Marshall could obtain no conference with a properly authorized plenipotentiary. On his arrival in January, he sent a note to Yeh, announcing his appointment and requesting an interview. He was far from pleased at Yeh's note of excuses.[39]   In his despatch to the Department of State[40] he gave vent to his indignation at being embarrassed in his usefulness, and announced his determination not to submit to such discourtesy. He then went to see Eliang (Governor of Kiang-nan and Kiang-si provinces), who received him in person on July 4, and sent to the Emperor the President's letter, and Marshall's request to be received at Peking to conduct American diplomatic relations there. He (Marshall) received acknowledgment of the letters, but his request was not granted. His hopes were chilled by new evasions and new reference to everything and everybody of Canton, the theatre of perplexity, and the usual channel for conducting diplomatic business. At Canton, however, all of his applications were refused.[41]

---

clouded their ideas of reform. They failed in their attack upon Peking, were expelled, by European powers, from Shanghai and Ningpo, and finally, in July, 1864, were driven from Nanking with merciless slaughter. The overthrow of the rebellion was aided by the leadership of Gen. Ward, an American, and Col. Gordon an Englishman.

[39] Yeh and the Governor returned the following gem of literary piquancy and Chinese diplomacy: " . . . We are delighted to understand that the honorable Commissioner has received the superintendence of trade at the five ports. We have heretofore heard that the honorable Commissioner is mild and even-tempered, just and upright. . . . As to setting a time for an interview, we, the Minister, and Governor are also exceedingly desirous of a mutual interview, when face to face we may converse, in order to manifest the good correspondence of our respective countries; but I, the Minister, am at present at Saou-Chow Pass, and I, the Governor, having the superintendence of everything, have not the slightest leisure, and can only await the return of the Minister. . . . ." [H. Exec. Doc. 123, 33-1, p. 13.]

[40] Despatch No. 3, Feb. 7, 1853.   H. Exec. Doc. 123, 33-1, p. 13.

[41] Despatches 21, 27, and 28, July 6, Aug. 26, and Aug. 30, 1853. H. Exec. Doc. 123, 33-1, pp. 189, 240, and 248.

He also had much difficulty and conflict with the American naval commanders, whom he asked to conduct him to northern ports, but to whom he refused to divulge his purposes in going. He complained that his exposure to the discourtesy of Commodore Aulick would leave an unfortunate impression on the minds of Chinese officials and result in the procrastination of impending questions and the loss of important advantages in political arrangements. With Perry, who relieved Aulick in the East, and stopped at Shanghai en route for Japan, he was no better pleased. Impatient in his desire to present his credentials, and to insist upon an official residence at Peking, and urging that it was a favorable time to press China for more satisfactory relations, he asked Perry [42] to leave a naval force at Shanghai to make his demands and negotiations more effective. [43] His proposition was disregarded. With no vessels at his command, and no prospects of diplomatic intercourse by the close of the year, he was not sorry to close his mission and return to the United States. The unreserved publication of his despatches (even of his most confidential letters) in July, 1854, gave the world an opportunity to see the extent and character of his vexations. His intention to leave China he

---

[42] Sen. Exec. Doc. 34, 33-2, pp. 23-26.

[43] In a note to Perry on May 13, Marshall said: " If the Emperor of China confronted by a formidable rebellion . . . would prefer to hazard war with the United States to an admission of their envoy to this court, yet will not execute his treaty obligations by appointing a proper public officer to adjust questions which arise in the foreign relations of his government, the United States might well desire to modify their policy with Japan until their future relations with China were more clearly ascertained."

In the latter part of the year, Perry who had returned to Hong Kong from Japan, was requested by Marshall to cooperate with him in an attempt to visit Peking to learn the exact condition of the revolution, to insist upon commercial rights, and to assure the " Christian Emperor " of his readiness to acknowledge the new government; but the Commodore, stating that neither of the Chinese parties was in a condition to negotiate, refused to take any step that might be interpreted as participation in the civil war.

announced to Yeh, who replied [January, 1854]: "I avail myself of the occasion to present my compliments, and trust that, of late, your blessings have been increasingly tranquil."

In October, 1853, Robert McLane was appointed Commissioner to China.[44] His instructions[45] of November 9, from Marcy, vested him with large and discretionary powers, by which he could be prepared to meet contingencies which might arise from the results of the existing revolution. He was directed, in case of a crisis, to attempt to secure unrestricted commercial intercourse—free trade, if possible—but with no desire for exclusive privileges.[46] He was assured that Perry would receive instructions to cooperate and give such assistance as the exigencies of the public interest might require, and at least to comply with any request for a steamer. In view of the possible success of the revolutionists, he was authorized to use his discretion in recognizing the government *de facto* and treat with it—or, in case China should be divided under several governments "promising stability," to negotiate treaties with each government.

Taking the overland route to the Pacific, McLane reached Hong Kong on March 13, 1854. Like his predecessor, he was unsuccessful in his attempts to open diplomatic intercourse. He found Yeh still too busy to talk.[47] Looking at

---

[44] Robert J. Walker had accepted the Chinese mission, but finally declined.

[45] Sen. Exec. Doc. 39, 36-1, vol. xi, Apr. 23, 1860. 4 pp.

[46] He was also given power to make a similar treaty with Corea, Cochin China, or any other independent Asiatic power with whom we had no treaty—and, in case Perry might fail, to renew efforts in Japan.

[47] On Apr. 6, Yeh in reply to McLane, wrote: "Yĕĕ . . . . am delighted to learn that the Commissioner has arrived in the south of China. . . . I, the Minister, am exceedingly comforted in my mind. As to appointing a time for presentation, I, the Minister, am also desirous of an interview . . . . ; but just at this moment, I the Minister, am superintending the affairs of the army in the several provinces, and day and night have no rest. Suffer me, then, to wait for a little leisure, when I may make selection of a propitious day, that we may have a pleasant meeting." [Sen. Exec. 22, 35-2, p. 19.]

the archives of the legation, he reported that they presented
a very humiliating view of our past relations with China,
whose officials rendered intercourse most unsatisfactory.
Considering the experience of both England and France,
he was convinced that diplomatic intercourse could be obtained with the Chinese Government only at the cannon's
mouth, but he resisted Sir John Bowring's suggestion for
uniting forces for combined action.[48]   Mr. Parker, secretary of the legation, suggested that the Chinese officials
should be warned that such discourteous treatment would
be borne no longer, and that a remonstrance should be presented to the emperor in person—either to Hèén Fung
or to Taiping.[49]

Informing Yeh that he would seek some other medium
of communication, McLane soon went northward to
Shanghai,[50] which had been held by the revolutionists since
the autumn of 1853, but was still annoyed by the imperial
forces. He found that American merchants were not yet
satisfied with the decision of Marshall, that suspension of
custom house control by the Imperial Government did not
annul the treaty obligation to pay duties.[51]   He sustained

---

[48] Despatch No. 3, to Marcy, Apr. 20, 1854. Sen. Exec. Doc. 22,
35-2, p. 21.

[49] In 1854, encouraged by the success of his Japan expedition,
Perry advocated the extension of the American policy (of stopping
exclusiveness) to Cambodia, Borneo, and especially to Formosa,
which he considered might be useful in aiding China to establish
a more liberal form of government. For the latter purpose he intimated that further intervention by Great Britain after the Opium
War would have been justifiable. Opposed to any toleration of
unsocial and insolent exclusiveness, he urged that diplomatic representatives should reside at Peking and other oriental capitals.
Looking to the future, he said: "We must protect commerce,
and prepare for events which must transpire, in the East. In the
developments of the future, the destinies of our nation must assume conspicuous attitudes." [Perry: U. S. Japan Expedition,
vol. ii, pp. 173-81.]

[50] Senate Exec. Doc. 22, 35-2 (vol. viii), p. 29 et seq. Despatch
Nos. 4, 5 and 6, May 4, and 21, and June 14, 1854.

[51] Marshall, considering that it was the duty of the United States
to protect the Chinese revenue, and that if duties were not paid

the decision of Marshall, however, and awarded to the Chinese the revenues due from Americans.[52]

In June, 1854, McLane visited Woohoo, about 70 miles above Nanking, and investigated the origin, purpose, and extent of the Taiping rebellion. The insurgent leaders appeared not to have the liberality and friendliness which had been attributed to them by the deluded missionary sympathizers. In exclusiveness and extraordinary pretensions the chiefs exceeded the tone of the imperial authorities.[53] They informed Captain Buchanan that he might be permitted to make yearly visits to bring tribute and bathe in the "gracious streams of the celestial dynasty."

In October, McLane, in company with Sir John Bowring, sailed northward, and after some "amphibious adventures" at the mouth of the Pei-ho, met an imperial [nonplenipotentiary] commissioner in a wretched tent near Taku, and participated in a fruitless conference which lasted almost an entire day.[54] On August 20, he had arrived at the conclusion that if the efforts then being made should

---

at Shanghai, they would be levied on the goods in the interior, had established a provisional arrangement for the payment or guarantee of the duties. The British residents did not favor the system, and offered no opposition to a "rebel" mob which sacked the custom house on September 7, 1853.

[52] Sen. Exec. Doc. 22, 35-2, p. 112 et seq. [Despatch 7, July 7, 1854.] On Nov. 8, before the award was paid over, Marcy agreeing with Lord Clarendon, gave instructions to rescind the arrangement as to duty obligations. Parker, the *chargé d'affaires* was much embarrassed by this order, and the insubordination of Mr. Murphy, the American consul. The question of paying the duties was finally settled by Attorney-General Cushing, who decided that the award of McLane, as an arbitrator, was obligatory. The Chinese difficulty in managing the revenues soon resulted in the establishment of a Foreign Inspectorate of Customs, to supervise the duties, and see that they were collected.

[53] See the "Mandatory" enclosed in Despatch No. 6 of June 14, 1854. Sen. Exec. Doc. 22, 35-2, p. 62. Also see p. 50 et seq., and p. 70 et seq.

[54] For Chinese memoranda of the conference, see enclosures in Reed to Cass, No. 33, Oct. 21, 1858, Sen. Exec. Doc. 30, 36-1, pp. 438-88 (vol. x).

prove unavailing, it would be necessary to abandon all further expectation of extending commercial intercourse by treaty, unless Great Britain and the United States should concur in a policy of exerting a more active and decided influence on the destiny of China.[55]   In November he urged Marcy to adopt a " more positive policy," stating that if the Chinese emperor remained obstinate a united Anglo-Franco-American fleet should blockade the Pei-ho, Yanste, Min, and Canton rivers, until all the commercial privileges demanded by the foreigners should be conceded.[56]

Secretary Marcy remained cool, conservative, and careful.

McLane having returned to the United States (in December, 1854) in poor health, in the summer of 1855 Mr. Parker was appointed commissioner.   His term of service was coincident with a period of troubles which severely tested his amiable, religious temper.   He went to China via London, where he exchanged generalities with Lord Clarendon on Anglo-Saxon interests, Anglo-American alliance, and " concurrent action and cooperation in China."

Like his predecessors, he failed to bring Yeh to a personal interview.   Unable to appreciate the latter's method of conducting the Chinese foreign office, he sailed northward.   On September 3, while at Shanghai, he wrote Marcy: " The contemplated plan of concurrent action on the part of Great Britain, France and the United States never appeared to me more wise or desirable than at this moment." [57]   Having no American squadron available to accompany him to the Pei-ho, he returned (November, 1856) to the south of China where he found American commercial interests paralyzed by the confusion resulting from the *Arrow* affair and the British bombardment of Canton.[58]

---

[55] Despatch No. 10, Sen. Exec. Doc. 22, 35-2, p. 169.
[56] Despatch 20, Nov. 19, 1854, Sen. Exec. Doc. 22, 35-2, p. 285.
[57] Sen. Exec. Doc. 22, 35-2, p. 921.
[58] Another effort to secure changes in treaties, which was about to be made in conjunction with the Ministers of France and England, was suspended by the Canton hostilities.

7

The United States was almost drawn into the conflict at Canton. A few Americans joined the British hostile forces and displayed the American flag. After the beginning of the conflict, the Chinese, having suggested the withdrawal of the American forces, became provoked because an American boat was sent "to sound the river in the vicinity of the forts" and they opened fire on a boat carrying the American flag, and belonging to one of the American ships-of-war. Commodore Armstrong, in reply, authorized a movement against the Barrier forts, then demanded an apology for the insult to the flag, and finally emphasized the demand by destroying the forts.[59] The British believed that the United States had become involved and would henceforth actively cooperate.[60]

Parker claimed to be cautious, but on December 12[61] he confidentially suggested to Marcy that the combined forces should present themselves at the Pei-ho, and in case China still refused to welcome envoys at Peking, as a final step resort to reprisal by hoisting the French flag in Corea, the British in Chusan, and the American in Formosa, and the retention of the territories until China should accept the terms offered, and give satisfaction for the past and a right

[59] Commanders Foote and Armstrong, notified by Consul O. H. Perry that there was danger of trouble, had moved up the river toward Canton for the purpose of protecting American citizens. The Chinese, excited by the collision with the British, fired upon the American vessels without cause. The action of the Americans in destroying the Barrier forts, was not regarded by the Chinese as an act of war, and was considered within the limits of a neutral policy. [H. M. Wood: Fankwei, N. Y., 1859.]

[60] Nearly a year later, Mr. Reed wrote Secretary Cass that the archives of the legation showed that Parker "to a certain point, encouraged Sir John Bowring [and others] in the most extravagant expectations of cooperation on our part, to the extent even of acquisition of territory." Referring to the mischievous effects of Parker's course he said that when the delusion was broken, and it became understood that the extreme policy of cooperation was disavowed, or discouraged, all suggestions of friendly concert on points of common interest, which the well-known policy of the government had authorized, were suddenly repelled. [Despatch 3, Reed to Cass, Nov. 10, 1857, Sen. Exec. Doc. 30, 36-1, vol. x, p. 17.]   [61] Despatch 34, Sen. Exec. Doc. 22, 35-2.

understanding for the future.[62]   He said that the occupation of territory, as a last resort, for injuries inflicted, would be far more humane and effective than the destruction of life and property by bombarding forts and cities.   On February 12, 1857, he again suggested the policy of taking Formosa.[63] He had just received a letter from Gideon Nye, Jr., who, considering the character of the mongrel race on the island, urged that Commodore Armstrong should take possession of the territory and hold it in the interests of humanity and commerce.[64]

Notwithstanding the attempt to involve the United States in hostilities, the American Government remained strictly neutral.   Secretary Marcy regretted that there had not been more caution by the Americans at Canton, and refused to entangle the United States in a protracted struggle.   " The British Government," said he, " evidently has objects beyond those contemplated by the United States, and we ought not to be drawn along with it, however anxious it may be for our cooperation." [65]   Considering that there was no obligation resting on China to negotiate at Peking, or near there, for the revision of the treaty of 1844, which she had agreed to revise, but without designating a place, the Pierce administration did not believe that relations with China warranted the " last resort " suggested by Parker. It decided to increase the naval force in Chinese waters, " but not for aggressive purposes." [66]

---

[62] Sen. Exec. Doc. 22 (part 2, p. 1083), 35-2.
In 1856 some urged that the United States, keeping up with England and France, should widen the area of her national institutions, maintain an imposing naval force in Chinese seas, and follow American commerce everywhere with a show of power. [H. M. Wood: Fankwei, or the San Jacinto in the Seas of India, China and Japan, N. Y., 1859.]   [63] Sen. Exec. Doc. 22, part 2, p. 1183.
[64] Ibid., Exhibit G, p. 1204.
[65] Instr. China, Marcy to Parker, No. 9, Feb. 2, 1857. In Sen. Exec. Doc. 30, 36-1, vol. x, p. 4.
[66] Instr. China, Marcy to Parker, No. 10, Feb. 27, 1857 [Ibid., p. 6]. In the following April Secretary Cass said: " We have of course no political views connected with that empire." [To Lord Napier, Apr. 10, 1857. In Sen. Exec. Doc. 47, 35-1.]

Secretary Cass, under the Buchanan administration, adhered to the same policy of neutrality. In March he received through Lord Napier a paper (dated January 9) from Lord Clarendon inviting the United States to join the alliance and participate in hostile movements against China in order to obtain the following objects:

1. Recognition of the right to send a minister to Peking.
2. Commercial extension beyond the five ports.
3. Reduction of tariff duties levied on domestic produce in transit from the interior.
4. Religious freedom of all foreigners in China.
5. An arrangement for the suppression of piracy.[67]
6. Provision for the extension of whatever benefits might be obtained to all other civilized powers of the earth.[68]

Though the President recognized all these objects as just and expedient, and was sensible of the liberal policy of the allied powers in disclaiming any intention to secure exclusive commercial advantages for themselves, he could not agree to cooperate in hostile demonstrations. Though he had power to employ naval forces for defence and for protection of American citizens, he stated that a military expedition into Chinese territory could not be undertaken except by Congress. Besides, although he was determined to ask China for a revision of the treaty of 1844 (which contained a clause providing for revision at the expiration of 12 years) he could not agree that our relations would warrant a resort to war. Secretary Cass, in his reply to Napier, said: " True wisdom dictates moderation and discretion in attempts to open China to the trade of the world." [69]

In May, Mr. William B. Reed was appointed [70] Envoy Ex-

---

[67] In 1855 a detachment from an American man-of-war destroyed the junks and burnt the depots of some pirates in Chinese waters. [Rp. Secy. of Navy, Dec. 1855.]

[68] MS. " Notes " from Brit. Legation to the Department, March 14, 1857.

[69] Notes from the Department to the Brit. Leg., Apr. 10, 1857.

[70] In July 1857, Parker, having no instructions, declined the invitation of the Earl of Elgin to unite with him in a visit to the

traordinary and Minister Plenipotentiary to China [to watch for an opportunity to revise treaties], with instructions [71] based upon a policy of peaceful cooperation in efforts to secure the objects sought by the allies.[72] " But on your side," said Cass, " efforts must be confined to firm representations, appealing to the justice and policy of the Chinese authorities, and [in case of failure] leaving to your own Government to determine upon the course to be adopted. . . . The United States is not at war with China, and only desires lawful commerce [73] and the protection of its citizens." The instructions explicitly stated that the United States had no motives of territorial aggrandizement or acquisition of political power in China.[74] Recognizing the potent influence of commerce alone as a means of introducing progressive civilization and national improvement, Cass said: " With the domestic institutions of China we have no political concern." Having no reason to believe that either of the contestants in the Chinese civil war would be more ready than the other to extend commercial intercourse, he directed Reed to use discretion in all that related to the internal conflict. To provide for possible contin-

---

north of China. In August, learning that Mr. Reed had been appointed to succeed him, he returned to the United States.

[71] Instr. China, Cass to Reed, No. 2, May 30, 1857. In Senate Exec. Doc. 47, 35-1, vol. xii, Apr. 20, 1858. (9 pp.)

[72] Reed was instructed that, in case Russia secured the reception of an accredited minister, there was no reason why he should not have the same friendly relations with the latter as with the British and French representatives.

[73] American citizens had not enjoyed " all the proper accommodations in obtaining homes and places of business," as provided by treaty. Local authority had interfered to prevent Chinese inhabitants from granting such rights, and had neglected to examine American complaints as to Chinese frauds or debts. They had not sufficiently enforced the guarantee of security for persons and property. The Chinese regulations reducing the true standard of the American coin had also injured trade.

[74] It was suggested that Mr. Reed, while watching for a favorable time to secure revision of treaties, might even have an opportunity to serve as a medium of communication between belligerents, and prevent war.

gencies the Chinese squadron was increased and the movement of forces placed as far as possible under Mr. Reed's control.

Mr. Reed, on reaching China, found the trade of all nations suspended by the blockade of the Canton river, and the imperial authorities still busy with the Taiping insurrection. He soon discovered that it was not a favorable time to negotiate for the revision of treaties.[75] On November 17 he wrote to the tranquil Yeh, announcing his arrival and requesting an interview. Before receiving a reply, he wrote again, on November 28, stating that the United States, although not a party to the existing hostilities, was determined to secure redress for wrongs which American citizens had suffered at the hands of Chinese authorities— and that friendly feeling could not possibly continue if China should withhold the courtesies of intercourse.[76] On November 24, Yeh replied that, although he had much desire for an interview, there was no place where to hold it, since the British had burned the houses near Canton. As to the treaty, he said it had " proved satisfactory " and needed no alterations. In December, he again wrote that the American merchants and citizens having been treated with courtesy and kindness in China, could have no wrongs to redress.[77] He expressed confidence that Reed, being clear-headed, would not act as Parker, whom he suggested had been recalled for his conduct. On December 12, Reed, regretting that no opportunity was given for an interview, the result of which might be beneficial to both nations, replied: "The time is not far distant when your excellency may be sorry you have not seen me. . . . The treaty of 1844 must be revised. . . . The time has come when the United States, the greatest nation of the Western world,

---

[75] Message of President Buchanan Dec. 8, 1857.

[76] In Despatch No. 36, Reed to Cass, Dec. 15, 1857. Sen. Exec. Doc. 30, 36-1, vol. x, pp. 49-53.

[77] Yeh to Reed, Dec. 8, 1857. Enclosure in Reed's No. 39 to Cass, Dec. 28.

must be treated on terms of equality with China, the oldest civilized nation of the East, and I have come in a conciliatory spirit to claim that right." In response, Yeh wrote (December 18): "From this it is plainly to be perceived that your excellency well understands the position of things, and the heartfelt regrets which you express have greatly tranquillized my feelings. . . . The despatches of . . . . Parker sometimes had remarks . . . not agreeable and courteous, but I never attached much importance to them in my mind. . . . Our two countries are like two good friends . . . in every respect on the best of terms." [78] Here the correspondence ended with the arrow of controversy still in the quiver. Such skillfully turned phrases and such masterly inactivity were difficult to meet by any form of literary retaliation known to the Western mind.

The crisis at Canton was rapidly approaching. By the close of the year all of the forts were taken. Early in January, 1858, Reed wrote that the city was completely in the hands of the allies. [79] Yeh had been captured and imprisoned on a war-vessel. At his house were found many documents relating to foreign affairs (including the original Cushing treaty), which indicated that the Foreign Office of China had practically been at Canton for many years. [80] On February 13, Yeh was sent to Calcutta for safe keeping. Having disposed of the tranquil commissioner, the powers prepared to urge their demands upon the Peking Government. Reed had come to the conclusion that vigorous action was necessary to secure redress. While suggesting

---

[78] Enclosure in Despatch 39, Reed to Cass, Dec. 28, 1857.

[79] "The Western powers," said Reed, "must give up the dream of dealing with China as a nation to which the ordinary rules apply." [Despatches, No. 3, Jan. 4, 1858. Sen. Exec. Doc. 30, 36-1, vol. x, p. 86.]

[80] Despatches, No. 5, Reed to Cass (Macao, Jan. 26, 1858). After learning more of these documents, which reflected the foreign policy of the Imperial Government, Reed wrote: "Decisive action is necessary with the officials who rule this people." [Despatches, No. 8, Feb. 4, 1858.]

that the Chinese indebtedness of $800,000 to the United
States might be realized by treaty, or by detention from
duties, he was confident that the only sure method of obtaining redress was peremptory demand enforced by the blockade of ports as a means of reprisal.[81]   By invitation, he coop-
erated with the allied powers and Russia in addressing
communications to Peking.   In his appeal to China he
stated that the United States, having most friendly relations
with Russia, France and Great Britain, and desiring the
integrity of China to remain inviolate by the terms of redress and peace, was ready to extend friendly offices.[82]   In
this appeal he was proud to unite, because he considered it
" entirely consistent with the peaceful attitude we have tried
to occupy in the East." [83]   He also considered that under his
instructions he could proceed with the allied fleets to the
north, and try the effect of the appearance of force near the
seat of the Imperial Government.   Desiring to provide for
a contingency in which China should refuse to negotiate
or resort to evasions, he asked to be invested with power to
resort to measures of coercion for securing redress.[84]

The Department of State approved Reed's course in joining the powers in writing the notes to the Chinese emperor, but stated that the United States could not join in a
continuation of coercive measures by resort to arms—at
least, not yet.[85]

The notes to Peking having failed to produce the desired
result, the powers decided to use more effective measures
by an advance toward the imperial capital.   Reed suggested that the United States should accompany the allied
fleet with all of her available force, to show the Oriental

---

[81] Despatches, No. 7, Feb. 1, 1858.   Sen. Exec. Doc. 30, 36-1, p. 104.

[82] For Reed's letter to the Chinese Government, see Sen. Exec. Doc. 30, 36-1, vol. x, pp. 171-75.

[83] Despatches, No. 9, Reed to Cass, Feb. 13, 1858.   Ibid., p. 125.

[84] The President had already asked Congress for such power.

[85] Instructions, China, No. 11, Cass to Reed, Apr. 28, 1858.

mind that she was not compelled to abstain from hostilities through any want of means.[86] In May, while preliminary operations were pending, he held conferences with Chinese commissioners, pursuing a course concerning which Lord Elgin guardedly expressed his dissent and disapproval.[87] He sailed with the allied fleet in their advance toward Peking, and was an observer of the hostilities which he had tried to prevent.[88] After the fleet had captured the Taku forts, enabling it to steam up the Pei-ho toward Peking and compel China to yield concessions, he secured all the advantages which had been forced by ball and bayonet. After several interviews with the Chinese commissioners at Tientsin, on June 18, he wrote: "I have to-day signed a treaty." In the negotiations, the two great points of difficulty were in regard to the permanent residence of a minister at Peking, and the navigation of the rivers.

The treaty, which Mr. Reed negotiated, renewed the extra-territoriality clause for consular judicial jurisdiction in suits against United States citizens in China, granted the right of direct correspondence with the privy council, permitted the minister of the United States to visit and sojourn at Peking for the transaction of business once each year, secured more liberal commercial regulations and gave access to new ports and to the interior of the country.[89] On No-

---

[86] Despatch No. 11, Reed to Cass, Shanghai, Apr. 3, 1858. A few days later, Reed seeing little chance of being able to accomplish anything, expressed a wish to return. On June 25 Cass replying that the President assented to his urgent wish, urged him to stay until there was no reasonable hope of prompt accommodation. [Instr. China, No. 12, Cass to Reed.]

[87] Despatch No. 17, Reed to Cass, May 15, 1858. Sen. Exec. Doc. 30, 36-1, vol. x, p. 297.

[88] The Russian and American squadrons were given orders to abstain from hostilities—except in cases of extremity.

[89] On the treaty and its effects, see Reed's despatch to Cass, No. 23, June 30, 1858. Sen. Exec. Doc. 30, 36-1, pp. 351-63, and 363-70; also despatch No. 29, July 29, 1858. Ibid., 371 et seq.

For further remarks on the treaty, and philosophic generalizations regarding the nature of the Chinese government and its foreign relations, the real authority in the political system, the Chi-

vember 8, he negotiated a convention[90] for settling the claims of American citizens, by which China afterwards paid the United States $735,238.97.[91]

The English and French treaties of 1858 each contained a clause providing for an exchange at Peking, and the envoys, Sir Frederick Bruce and M. de Bourbillon, refused to listen to Chinese officials who were sent to Shanghai to dissuade them from going to Peking.[92]   Arriving at the mouth of the Pei-ho in June, 1859, they found the river obstructed by improved forts at Taku and, by chains which the Chinese refused to remove.   The allied fleet of nineteen vessels was under the command of the English admiral, Hope.   Upon learning of the obstructions in the river, Admiral Hope made an imperative demand that they be removed at once. This the Chinese refused, and Bruce, hoping that the matter was susceptible of an amicable adjustment, attempted to enter into negotiations for the removal of the booms so that he might be permitted to pursue his journey to Peking.

Almost coincident with the arrival of the British and French, two American vessels, under Commander Josiah Tatnall, escorting the American Minister, John E. Ward, reached the waters of the Pei-ho.   Ward had received the assent of the Chinese commissioners at Shanghai to go to the imperial capital, and had resolved to proceed until stopped by a force which could not be overcome by that under Tatnall by which he was escorted.   Persuaded by

---

nese negotiations, and the influence of the conduct of foreigners, see Reed's despatch No. 31 to Cass, Sept. 4, 1858.   Ibid., p. 429 et seq.

For illustrations of Chinese polity, and characteristics, see D. Wells Williams's despatch No. 2 to Cass, Jan. 28, 1859.   Ibid., p. 545.

[90] Despatches, Nos. 35 and 37, Reed to Cass, Nov. 9, and Nov. 10, 1858.   Ibid., pp. 493-528.

[91] After the settlement of the claims by a United States commission, a surplus remained.   In 1885 a balance of $453,400.90 was returned to the Chinese minister at Washington.

[92] See 14 Ward to Cass June 13, 1859.   Sen. Exec. Doc. 30, 36-1, pp. 569-85.

Tatnall, on June 25 he boarded an American chartered steamer, which passed the vessels of the allies, but grounded on a mud flat when within half a mile of the forts. On the next day, after the American vessel had been floated out of the line of fire, the allies began the attack on the yellow-flag-crowned Taku forts and attempted to clear the river, but the Chinese, with more artillery than had been suspected, opened a heavy fire which did serious damage. Throughout the fight the American force was nominally neutral. But Tatnall, when a young British officer informed him that Admiral Hope was seriously wounded, and intimated that American assistance would relieve the situation, turning to Ward, said: " I must either help Hope or return to the *Powhatan*. I can't stand here and see them shot to pieces. . . . Blood is thicker than water." He proceeded to extend his sympathy, and despite the protests of fellow-officers, assisted in landing men from the allied fleet to storm the forts. When the landing party was cut to pieces he sent boats to aid them to return to their vessels.[93]

After the fight made it evident he could not reach Peking with the French and English, Ward, in accordance with treaty provisions, opened negotiations for means of conveyance overland.[94] In a yellow cart, he started toward the imperial city, and on August 16, without force, secured the ratification of the treaty.[95]

---

[93] Sen. Exec. Doc. 30, pp. 585-91.   15 Ward to Cass, July 4, 1859.
[94] Ibid., pp. 591-94.   16 Ward to Cass, July 10, 1859.
[95] Ibid., p. 594 et seq.   17 Ward to Cass, Aug. 20, 1859. Ward landed at Pei-t'ang, north of the mouth of the Pei-ho, and was taken to Peking by carts and by boats, over which floated a yellow pennant with the words: "Tribute bearer from the United States." The imperial commissioners informed him that it was necessary to have an audience with the emperor before the treaty could be exchanged, but agreed to require of him only one-third of the usual number of kneelings (three) and touchings of the head on the ground (nine) required of envoys. Ward replied that he knelt only to God, and refused to bow except as he would to the President of the United States. The commissioners then arranged a plan for avoiding the formalities, but the emperor insisted that he

The Chinese continued to oppose the treaties after they had been ratified, and endeavored to prevent their execution.[96] In 1860 British and French forces, having destroyed the defences of the Pei-ho river, took possession of the imperial city and induced the opening of the new ports of Nin-Chwang, Tung-Chan, Tai-wan (in Formosa), Chan-Chau, Kiang-Chau and (later) Tientsin. Russia, taking occasion to settle long-standing questions, obtained from China the region north of the Amoor and a tract along the coast of Manchuria below 43°.

Burlingame, whom Seward sent as United States minister to China in June, 1861, with instructions to lend no aid or countenance to the Taiping rebellion, but to consult with English and French ministers, desired the treaty powers to agree on the neutrality of China, to secure order in the treaty ports,[97] give their moral support to the Chinese party which was in favor of order, to encourage the adoption of progressive reforms and make an effort to substitute diplomatic action for force. His ideas met with the approval of the representatives of Great Britain, France and Russia. Some foreigners, however, advocated alienation of Chinese

---

must touch either the knee or the fingers to the ground, and no audience was arranged. The ratified treaties were unceremoniously exchanged at Pei-t'ang where Ward embarked for Shanghai.

A. A. Hayes, in an article in the Atlantic Monthly for May, 1887, says that it has been our policy to "crawl behind the British guns, and come forward at the end of war with our bills for lost dressing-gowns, pipes, slippers and peace of mind."

[96] While an Anglo-French war against China was impending in Feb., 1860, President Buchanan agreed that the United States should pursue the same policy as that outlined by Russia.

[97] In several cases American naval forces had aided in preserving order. In August, 1859, during a disturbance which arose among the Chinese population at Shanghai on account of alleged kidnapping of "coolies" for a French merchant vessel, Captain Nicholson, at the request of the United States consul, landed part of his crew of the *Mississippi*, but order was restored and no collision occurred. [Rp. Secy. of Navy, Dec., 1859.] In June, 1860, during a fight between the Canton Chinchew men, Commander Berrien, at request of Consul Gouverneur, sent an armed boat to protect American residents.

territory at the principal treaty ports and exclusive jurisdiction by England; and others, though well-meaning, excited the opposition of the Chinese by pressing the question of constructing railways and telegraphs.

In 1868, Burlingame, as minister plenipotentiary of China, negotiated a treaty with the United States favoring the territorial integrity of the empire, exempting persons from persecution for religious faith, acknowledging the right of voluntary emigration,[98] and confirming the previous consular jurisdiction. Though Secretary Fish thought the United States should have additional concessions, and that there should be a moderation of the restrictions which fettered commerce, he had no desire to embarrass the Chinese Government.[99]

In her subsequent relations with China the United States has continued to be non-aggressive, modest and friendly. She has continued to adhere to a policy of cooperation with the other powers upon the principle of native independence, an open door, and equality of opportunity for all the powers concerned. Notwithstanding her Chinese exclusion laws,

---

[98] The United States had aided China to suppress the Coolie trade, but had found it very difficult to prevent the emigration of Chinese under false pretences, so long as they were prohibited from leaving the country freely. [See Sen. Exec. Doc. 22, 35-2, p. 657.]

[99] In 1870 President Grant concurred with the opinion of Germany that the combined action of the powers should end piracy in Chinese waters. In 1871, when there were unsettled questions growing out of Chinese opposition to Christianity, some urged measures that would teach China a lesson which she would long remember. In 1867-69 there had been local outrages against foreigners. A crisis was reached by the massacre at Tientsin. France asked redress. China prevaricated and delayed, then promised to pay an indemnity, and finally refused to pay, demanded the abolition of schools for the education of females, and insisted that males should not be taught doctrines opposed to those of Confucius. She also desired to consider missionaries as Chinese subjects, and to prevent the access of women to the empire in that capacity. *The Nation* (Aug. 17, 1871) urged that the United States, though not engaged in religious propagandism, should not hesitate to use force, or to unite with other powers, if necessary, to induce China to recede from her position.

she has always stood well at Peking. Her efforts in behalf of an open door are regarded as distinctly in the interest of the integrity of the Chinese Empire. Her influence in the Orient has been greatly increased by the occupation and acquisition of the Philippines. In case the other powers, by their rivalry and spheres of influence in China, should attempt a policy of partition, she probably would not allow treaty rights and general interests to be sacrificed to such schemes of aggrandizement. She might even call in the Monroe doctrine in defence of her course.

Secretary Hay, on entering upon the duties of Secretary of State, saw that the inevitable retention of the Philippines would enable the United States to secure her policy in China and the East. After signing the treaty of Paris, he took steps to obtain from foreign powers, having " spheres of influence " in China, a recognition of our treaty rights to an open door. Some of the powers intimated that instead of a written assurance they would allow the United States a " sphere of influence," but Hay refused to participate in the partition policy. While avoiding an alliance with England or a treaty with any of the powers respecting a policy in China, he has insisted that the foreign powers, by treaties with each other and with China, should give a written guarantee of an open door.

In the recent Chinese crisis, while cooperating with the allies in the advance against Peking, to protect the foreign legations, the United States has had no territorial designs. She desires an open door to the trade of all China, and not a restricted sphere of influence over any part of it. She consistently strives for the larger field of commercial opportunity unlimited by territorial boundaries. If, through her prestige as a territorially disinterested power, she can prevent partition, restore peace to the Empire, and be assured of the protection of American rights and lives, she will have the reward or compensation which comes from the performance of duty by a necessary activity which has left our traditions unendangered.

Corea.[100]—Corea, with a policy of exclusion and inclusion, remained for ages in a state of seclusion. About the beginning of 1868, Frederick Jenkins, an American, who had served as interpreter at the United States consulate at Shanghai, sailed to Corea on the *General Sherman* with an expedition which he had organized to rob the tombs of the deceased Corean sovereigns as a means of securing a ransom. The conduct of some of the crew on landing excited the Coreans to kill eight of them and destroy their vessel. The Corean Government, desiring to explain the circumstances connected with the affair, and contemplating the expediency of securing a treaty of friendship and commerce, in April, 1868, sent commissioners to Mr. Seward, the United States consul-general at Shanghai, for consultation.

After considerable correspondence, and with the assurance from the Peking Government that Corea's tributary relation to China did not prevent her from making treaties, F. F. Low, United States Minister to China, accompanied by Mr. Seward and Rear-Admiral Rodgers, with a squadron of five vessels, went to Corea in April, 1871, by instructions from Washington, and made an attempt to negotiate a convention securing rescue and protection to our shipwrecked mariners and property.[101] They arrived in the Salu river April 25, and on May 29, in a friendly manner, informed the officials of their purpose to continue up the river to make surveys. The officials made no objection to the surveys, but said the king was averse to making treaties. On June 1 several surveying vessels were fired upon from forts, which they soon silenced. The Coreans stubbornly refusing to offer an apology, on June 10 an expedition of nearly 1000 men, sent to avenge the insult, destroyed forts and batteries and killed 253 Coreans, who were then glad to fall back.

---

[100] W. E. Griffis: Corea: the hermit nation. 1882.

[101] President's Message of Dec. 1871, and accompanying documents.

[102] Pamphlet at Navy Department, on "Expedition to Corea, 1871."

Before leaving, Low made another attempt to open negotiations with the Government, but the letter to the king was returned unopened, and he was informed that no one dare convey his letter to Seoul. Rodgers, after further efforts appeared useless, went to Chefoo to await orders from the United States. Though the expedition had only contemplated peaceful negotiations, some hoped the powers would take united action against this warlike people; but the Washington Government, seeing no hope of accomplishing anything without a display of force, decided to postpone further negotiations.

After the bloodless revolution of 1874, which deposed a tyrannical usurping ruler, the Coreans became more interested in foreign nations and better acquainted with their policies; and, after a war with Japan, which opened several ports to Japanese commerce, notwithstanding ancient laws, they began to visit other countries. Secretary Frelinghuysen, seeing favorable conditions for renewing negotiations, and considering that the independence of Corea was regarded as established, resolved again to make an effort to obtain a treaty with the land of the Morning Calm, and intrusted the delicate mission to Admiral Shufeldt, who, on May 22, 1882, concluded a treaty securing the opening of certain ports to our commerce, aid and protection to our vessels and seamen, and safety to our citizens while in Corea. Lucius H. Foote, who, in May, 1883, became the first United States minister to Corea, made a favorable impression as to the friendly purposes of the American government, and relations since have been cordial and harmonious.

For 2000 years Corea has had a government based on the spoils system. In the almost thirty centuries during which she has patiently played a negative part, trying to steer between the Scylla of China and the Charybdis of Japan, she has been buried beneath a mass of worn-out, alien (Chinese) ideals—legal, religious and social—which have almost crushed her spontaneity. She cannot be exhumed, disinterred, and reclaimed without a process of education. In the riot of December, 1884, some of the liberals inaugurated a hurricane of reform which lasted for forty-eight hours, but they failed in the attempt to condense centuries of evolution into a few hours.[108] The need of reforms in the administration and finances of Corea furnished an occasion for the events which caused the recent Chino-Japanese war, since which a reaction has largely transferred to Russia the influence previously exerted by Japan in Corea; but Japan expects to be a dominant force in guiding the destiny of both Corea and China.

---

[108] Foreign Relations, 1885. Percival Lowell: "The coup d'état in Corea." Atlantic Monthly, vol. lviii, 1886.

CHAPTER VIII.

AMERICANIZATION OF HAWAII.

The interests which the United States suddenly acquired in California, the development of Oregon, and the prospects of closer communication with Asia, increased the importance of the earlier American policy to prevent foreign colonization or control of the Hawaiian Islands, where American elements had predominated from the earliest days of foreign interests there, and led the American Government to contemplate the annexation of the islands as a possible contingency necessary to American interests.

American influence in the islands was considerable by 1820. In March of that year, missionaries from Boston arrived in the *Thaddeus* to begin their religious and humanitarian work, and in the following September President Monroe appointed John C. Jones as United States agent, for commerce and seamen at Hawaii, to make reports to the Department of State. The missionaries were hospitably received and found conditions favorable for their labors. Kamehameha I., the " Napoleon of the Pacific," who, by 1795, had practically asserted his control over all the septinsular kingdom, had died in 1819, leaving a consolidated kingdom to his son Liholiho, who succeeded him as Kamehameha II. The will of the chief was still almost absolute. There had not yet developed a code of laws, or government regulations, courts of justice, or the acknowledged right of persons to own property. Neither was there yet a written or systematized language. But the people were preparing to be transformed by the institutions of civilization. Under the influence of foreigners, they became infidels to the old religion. After disobeying old religious rites they found that their health was as good as before. Under Liholiho, "tabu" and idolatry were abolished by law.[1]

The missionaries, who soon exerted considerable influence with the native government, were opposed by foreigners, who finally led the king into dissipation and debts which caused him to increase taxes. Richard Charlton, the British consul-general at Hawaii, was accused of placing himself at the head of the lawless and depraved class of foreigners, and trying to induce the chiefs to make no laws without the approval of the British Government.[2] He showed an open antagonism to the American missionaries and American influence on the islands, tried to organize the discordant elements into an anti-missionary party, and, later, he favored the introduction of a rival religion by French Catholic priests, who were appointed by the Pope in 1826. The Hawaiian Government remained friendly to the Protestant missionaries, and in April, 1831, issued a decree banishing the Jesuits; it was inclined to persecute those who had embraced the Roman faith, though the severity of the persecution was lessened by a visit of the *Potomac* in 1832.[3]

Toward the close of 1832 political troubles increased. The

---

[1] J. J. Jarvis: History of the Sandwich Islands.

[2] In 1823 Liholiho, suspecting Russia of having designs, decided to ask England and the United States for protection and visited London, where he died, and from whence his remains were conveyed to Honolulu in the *Blonde* under the command of Lord Byron. [G. A. Byron: Voyage of the *Blonde* to the Sandwich Islands, 1824-5. London, 1826.] George IV. promised protection against foreign aggression. British influence had long before shown itself. In February, 1793, Vancouver, returned to the islands and endeavored to secure an end to the internal dissensions that were reducing the population. A year later, a meeting of the great chiefs decided to cede Hawaii to England as a protectorate, and Mr. Puget went ashore, hoisted the British colors and took possession.

[3] About the same time a writer in the London Metropolitan Magazine proposed that the British Government should take possession of the islands as a matter of expediency. [J. N. Reynolds: Voyage of the *Potomac*, p. 416.]

young King Kamehameha III., partly through the influence
of Charlton, had thrown off the restraints of his elders and
abandoned himself to dissipation and debauchery.   He asso-
ciated with the licentious, and delegated his royal power to
Kaomi, an unprincipled Tahitian.   Shameless dances were
revived, family ties were sundered, and drunkenness ruled.
Kinau, the eldest sister of Kamehameha I., stood for decency, but she could not obtain the ear of the king.[4]

In July, 1839, Captain Laplace, of the French frigate
Artemise, forced Kamehameha III. to allow the return of
the priests, the entire freedom of Catholic worship, and the
introduction of intoxicating liquors into the islands.   Many
priests now came, and trouble soon arose between them
and the Protestants.   French and English grievances continued.

In 1842 a French vessel arrived with new demands, to
which the king replied that he had sent an embassy to
France to negotiate a treaty.   The English consul, Charlton, also presented a list of grievances,[5] causing the king
(July, 1842) to ask for his removal and to send a communication to the United States, England and France to negotiate new treaties and obtain a guarantee of independence
and neutrality.

Notwithstanding the reports of progress in the islands
and the increase of American interests there, the United
States sought no exclusive control or advantage, but desired that American rights should be respected and guarded.
Webster, in his reply to the Hawaiian commissioners, stated
that the government of Hawaii should not be an object of
interference by foreign powers,[6] but advised them to begin
diplomatic operations in England.

---

[4] Laura Fish Judd: Honolulu, etc., 1828-61. N. Y., 1880.

[5] Charlton had a title to some Hawaiian lands, and claimed the
right to transfer it, but the courts of Hawaii decided against him
and attached his land. Though the Government made no attempt to
eject him from the lands, he claimed that his rights had been in-
fringed, and complained to the British Government.

[6] Wilkes, who visited the islands on his exploring expedition,
said: "Fortunately for the Sandwich Islands they have no port

Desiring to defeat the objects of the embassy, Charlton secretly went to England, leaving a hostile deputy, Simpson, whom the king refused to recognize until he was forced to do so by Lord George Paulet, of the British navy, who arrived February 10, 1843, threatened the authorities, took possession of the islands under the British flag,[7] seized all lands claimed by Charlton, abrogated laws against vice, and raised an army of natives. The king, after executing the forced cession, wrote President Tyler, protesting and asking the United States to interpose.

The United States, when informed of this affair by the communication from the Hawaiian king, declared that no power ought to take possession of the islands either as a conquest or for colonization.[8] She took steps, through Everett, to notify England that the United States would regret if England or France should adopt any other than a pacific, just and conservative course toward Hawaii. The attitude of the United States doubtless influenced England and France to recognize Hawaiian independence and (November 28, 1845) to enter into a joint declaration agreeing never to take possession even under a protectorate. England promised to remove Charlton, and a few years later France restored $20,000 that had been extorted by the French captain in 1839.

---

that is defensible against a strong naval force, and therefore their importance will be comparatively small in a political point of view. No foreign power, in fact, could well hold them without great expense and difficulty. . . . They will no doubt be left in the enjoyment of their neutrality. . . . It is the interest of the United States that they should maintain the neutrality that they seek to establish." [C. Wilkes: Voyage Around the World, 1838-43. N. Y., 1851.]

[7] In July, however, the British admiral, Thomas, arriving, disapproved the acts of his ambitious subordinate, refused to accept the cession of the islands, and proceeded to restore the king. Although France had recently seized the Marquesas, the British Government disavowed the seizure and cession of Hawaii.

[8] On June 13, 1843, Legare wrote Everett that the United States might feel justified in interfering by force to prevent Hawaii falling, by conquest, into the hands of one of the great powers of Europe.

In March, 1843, the United States Government, feeling the need of a competent medium of communication and of closer and more friendly relations, appointed George Brown, of Massachusetts, as a diplomatic official. The latter was well received, but soon had occasion to insist that Americans accused of crime should have the right of trial by a jury composed entirely of foreigners, and to protest that the British treaty of February, 1844, discriminated against the United States. He was recalled at the request of the Hawaiian king. Mr. A. Ten Eyck, who succeeded him in 1846, with instructions to make a treaty, continued to insist upon the right of trial by a jury of foreigners until, in 1848, feeling that relations were on the point of rupture, and that President Polk had neglected him, he resigned, and was succeeded by Charles Eames. Before the latter reached Hawaii, Mr. J. J. Jarvis and Secretary Clayton, at Washington, had concluded a treaty of friendship, commerce, navigation and extradition (December 20, 1849), which was ratified by the United States Senate the following February, exchanged in August and proclaimed in November.[9]

Foreign consular and diplomatic representatives continued to threaten interference with internal affairs of Hawaii. England revived old claims. The French consul reopened old disputes and presented new ones, causing the king to ask his recall. In August, 1849, a French frigate arrived to support the demands of the consul. Against the urgent protests of English and American consuls, a French force, under pretext that provisions of the French-Hawaiian treaty had been broken, seized buildings, destroyed property, blockaded the harbor and took the king's yacht. The admiral had notified the United States consul, Turrell, that the French desired only reparation, and had no designs

---

[9] Andrew H. Allen: Relations between the United States and the Hawaiian Islands 1820-93. [Sen. Exec. Doc. 77, 52-2, Feb. 17, 1893.]

for occupation or protectorate, and he had neither lowered the Hawaiian flag nor raised that of France. The king, through Turrell, again invoked the good offices of the United States to maintain his sovereignty, and sent J. J. Jarvis as special commissioner to procure the friendly mediation of President Fillmore. Secretary Clayton, uncertain whether France would adopt the same policy with Hawaii as with Tahiti, wrote Rives at Paris that, although the Hawaiian Islands were not coveted by the United States, their relations were such that the United States could never with indifference allow them to pass under the dominion or exclusive control of any other power. Later, the French Government disavowed the action of its admiral, but on learning that a commission had gone to the United States and England to make new treaties, sent out a counter commission to renew the old demands. A French vessel arrived December 13, 1850, and remained three months to harass and interfere.

In March, 1851, Severance wrote Webster that the popular representative body recently elected by the native votes, and also the executive and judiciary, were composed largely of natives of the United States; that the king and his government, fearing France, were privately considering the subject of annexation to the United States, and that a United States ship-of-war should be present to prevent the fear of disturbances which had operated to injure American commerce, immigration and land-purchases. He said that the Americans who had opposed the government and the missionaries, on account of laws against licentiousness and drunkenness, were decreasing in number, and would join the missionaries in rallying under the United States flag should it once be raised. Judging from foreign relations and the precarious state of the king's health, he was uncertain whether the native government could last long. Seeing the value of Hawaii, with her public lands and no public debt, and with proposed steam communication with San Francisco, which could be connected with Washington by telegraph, he hoped that Webster would not object to a political connection on account of distance.

On March 10, 1851, the king and privy council of Hawaii issued a proclamation placing Hawaii under the protection of the United States, and on June 21 the provisional cession was adopted by both Houses of the Hawaiian Parliament. Webster, however, on July 14, directed Severance to return the deed to the Hawaiian Government. He still advocated the past policy of favoring the independence of the islands, at least until pressed by some necessity in which events should occur to give the subject a new aspect and an increased importance. Referring to Americans who were settling in Hawaii, he informed Severance that they thereby ceased to be citizens of the United States, saying: " You will, therefore, not encourage in them, nor indeed in any others, any idea or expectation that the islands will become annexed to the United States. All this will be judged of hereafter as circumstances and events may require by the government at Washington." The United States, however, faithful to its original assurances, scrupulously regarded the independence of the islands and was unwilling to consent that European powers should occupy them or enforce unjust demands inconsistent with their independence. The Navy Department received instructions to keep the Pacific armament in a position requisite for the preservation of the honor and dignity of the United States and the safety of the government of Hawaii.

France, checked in her plans, expressed surprise at the American attitude, and disclaimed any intention of improper interference, or of assuming sovereignty in the islands.

The increasing American influence in Hawaii [10] excited

---

[10] Feeling that the United States had become an arbiter in the affairs of the Pacific, a writer in De Bow's Magazine, in November, 1852, asked whether Hawaii, who requested our protection, was not as necessary to the United States as Cuba.

the jealousy of both France and England. In September, 1853, Secretary Marcy, while disclaiming any intention of the United States to exercise exclusive control, indicated that she would not allow other powers to exact special polit-ical or commercial privileges, or to establish a protectorate over the islands.[11] In the following December, while hop-ing to acquire Lower California, he informed the American minister to France that the existing condition of the islands made it appear inevitable that they must come under the control of the United States. Sailor riots, filibustering ex-peditions from California and internal strife and the de-mands and threats of the British and French had caused a rising annexation sentiment at Honolulu.

Being informed that the British and French would forcibly resist a transfer of the islands to the United States,[12] Marcy (December 16) instructed Mr. Mason, at Paris, to sound the French Government upon its policy or views. Feeling that the Hawaiian Islands could not long remain under the existing rulers, or under the control of the inhab-itants, and that their geographical position and their con-nection with Pacific industries in which American interests were paramount[13] would inevitably result in their control by the United States Government, he urged that it would be fair for England and France to acquiesce in any transfer made to the United States by fair means.

While the United States had long expressed her policy of maintaining the independence of the Hawaiian Islands, she had never entered into any international agreement which would prevent her from negotiating a treaty of an-nexation with the Hawaiian Government. She was free to encourage any movement originating in Hawaii.[14] In

[11] Instr. Hawaii, Sept. 22. Marcy to Gregg.

[12] He also had an intimation that Russia had an eye on the islands, but had little fear of interference from that quarter.

[13] 650 vessels were at this time engaged in whaling, and mostly in the Pacific.

[14] Washburn of Me., on Jan. 4, 1854, made a speech in Congress, in which he favored expansion to include Hawaii. 29 Con. Globe, 33-1, Appendix, pp. 55-59.

February, 1854, Marcy received a letter from Minister Gregg stating that the king, fearing his inability to maintain the independence of the islands, had made advances indicating that he might offer to transfer the sovereignty to the United States. On April 4 he authorized Gregg, whenever the emergency should arise, to negotiate for a complete transfer of the islands to the United States as a *territorial possession,* and suggested that $100,000 might be given to the chiefs as compensation for losses which they would sustain.

Negotiations were opened with the Hawaiian authorities, who soon showed an " inveterate prejudice against a territorial form of government," and, after approving a form of treaty, secured delay by urging the necessity of consulting the king, who was ill.[15] Gregg, fearing a crisis, desired prompt negotiations and immediate transfer, believing that after the cession, provisional or permanent, was once made the flood of emigration from California would soon follow the raising of the American flag, Americanize the islands, and check future British and French pretensions.

In September the king seemed satisfied with the proposed form of treaty, but the British[16] and French consuls at Honolulu protested, and the admirals of a combined British and French squadron warned the king that a cession to the United States would lead to difficulty. The king proceeded with the negotiations, but insisted until he obtained clauses securing additional compensation, and providing that the islands should be admitted as a State of the Union.[17] On

---

[15] Gregg to Marcy, Aug. 7, 1854.

[16] Gregg said that publications in the *New York Tribune* of July 20, unfortunately aided the British in their attempts to prejudice the Hawaiians against the American policy of Marcy and Gregg. (September 15, 1854.)

[17] Marcy felt that the Senate would never approve the clause providing for statehood in the Union; but, on January 31, 1855, he instructed Gregg that the United States Government was willing to receive the transfer of the sovereignty of the islands with all provisions as to the rights of the inhabitants, and would desire their prosperity.

September 18, General Miller, the British consul-general, strongly deprecating annexation, urged the king not to execute the treaty.[18] The latter remained friendly to the United States, but died (December 15) while negotiations for the final execution of the treaty were still pending.

Kamehameha IV., who became king on January 11, 1855, became opposed to the completion of the treaty, and was probably influenced by the English relationship of Emma Rooke, who, in 1856, became Queen Emma. In 1855 he participated in the negotiations of a treaty of reciprocity which the United States afterwards failed to ratify. Until his death (November, 1863) he remained strongly predisposed to favor the British in preference to the Americans. The latter began to suspect that British diplomacy was preparing Hawaii for a British regency at the death of the king, with the intention of making it a cotton-growing colony.

Notwithstanding the decline of the whale fisheries after 1854, and the growing influence of the British with the Hawaiian royal family, American influence in the islands was kept alive through the channels of industry. In 1857 more than one-half the imports at Honolulu were from the United States. In 1863, four-fifths of the commerce connected with the islands was American. Interest was increased by the rise of the sugar industry [19] which, at the close of the American civil war, became the basis for the agitation of a treaty of reciprocity with the United States.

On October 9, 1863, Minister McBride, commenting upon the extensive American commercial and sugar interests in the islands, wrote Seward that their control by the United States Government would be "far more valuable than the ownership of both Cuba and the Bahama Islands." His successor, Edward M. McCook, on September 3, 1866, informed Secretary Seward that, although many of the American residents were dissatisfied with the king and cabinet,

---

[18] Gregg to Marcy, Oct. 2, 1854.
[19] Settlers had cultivated sugar cane at a very early day, and, by 1853, they were planting nearly 3000 acres.

the influence of the American Government, so far as he could see, was " all that it had ever been," and that the spirit of the people was " heartily republican and thoroughly American." Suggesting that the king would probably die at an early date without a successor, and that the arbitration of the destiny the country would devolve upon the United States, he added " And when this dynasty ends ... I am sure that if the American Government indicates the slightest desire to test in their islands the last Napoleonic conception in the way of territorial extension, you will find the people here with great unanimity demanding by votes, freely expressed, annexation to the United States."

On May 21, 1867, McCook, by written invitation of the Hawaiian Government, negotiated a treaty of reciprocity which was more liberal than that of 1855. The king, probably by the advice of Varigny, who was his minister of foreign affairs, objected to the presence of the United States ship *Lackawanna* in Hawaiian waters, and delayed the ratification of the treaty. After the departure of the vessel, he convened the legislature and approved the treaty on July 30. Three days later he sent Captain Waterman as an envoy to Japan to attempt negotiations for a commercial treaty—a project which McCook urged would defeat the objects of the treaty with the United States by diverting into another channel the trade we wished to secure,[20] and decreasing our commercial and political influence on the islands.

McCook regarded the treaty of reciprocity as a means of making American influence dominant on the islands and in line with a policy of future annexation. President Johnson, stating that there was a growing conviction that our constitutional system is strong enough to comprehend possessions beyond the continent,[21] considered the treaty a guar-

---

[20] He desired to secure all of the trade of China and Japan as well as that of Hawaii. McCook to Van Valkenburg, Aug. 3, 1867.

[21] The establishment of a regular steamer service between San Francisco and China in 1867 shortened the communication between the United States and Hawaii. Previous communication had been by whale ships via Cape Horn.

antee of foreign forbearance in Hawaii until the people of the islands should voluntarily apply for admission into the Union. There were some who opposed reciprocity on the ground that it would " hinder and defeat early annexation," but this probably does not explain the motive of the Senate, which rejected the treaty after delaying action until June 1, 1870.

On July 13, 1867, Secretary Seward authorized McCook (at the latter's own suggestion) to sound the Hawaiian authorities on the subject of annexation; to ascertain the probable conditions and confidentially to receive overtures. In the following September he wrote him that lawful and peaceful annexation of the islands, with the consent of the people there, was desired, and that in case of any conflict between the policy of reciprocity and that of annexation the latter was " in every case to be preferred." In the summer of 1868 he was informed that the annexation sentiment in Hawaii was so strong that immediate occupation, under some pretext of defending American rights, would hardly raise a single remonstrance; but he saw that the public mind was so much fastened on domestic questions (reconstruction) that it would hardly entertain " the higher but more remote questions of national extension and aggrandizement," and prudently avoided giving encouragement to the Hawaiian-American annexationists.

On September 14, 1869, in the course of a confidential conversation with the King of Hawaii, McCook stated that the United States, needing a naval depot between the Pacific coast and China, probably would be willing to pay a liberal price for the cession of any or all of the islands; but the king said it was not the policy of the government to cede either of the four larger islands, and that the United States would have no use for the smaller ones which had no harbors.

On February 25, 1871, Mr. Henry A. Pierce, United States minister at Honolulu, wrote to Fish suggesting that it was a favorable time to secure the political destiny of

Hawaiian Islands by annexation to the United States. In support of this policy, he said the majority of aborigines, creoles, and the democratic New England settlers, were anxious for annexation; that the fifteenth amendment to the United States Constitution had increased the popularity of the project; that the strategical position of the islands for a naval or coaling station, and for the protection of United States commerce in the Pacific was an important consideration; and that His Hawaiian Majesty, whose fatness made his breathing difficult, was likely to die from suffocation without leaving a successor to the throne. President Grant, who was urging the annexation of San Domingo, confidently referred this despatch to the Senate and invited an expression of its views, but he did not obtain the encouragement necessary to enable him to express the policy of the Government upon the subject.

In February, 1873, as a means of removing Hawaiian lukewarmness and fear of repulse, Pierce urged an expression of the American policy. Though he thought annexation probably would never be presented or adopted as a measure of the Hawaiian Government, he said that the planters, merchants and foreigners, whenever great interests required it, would induce the people to establish a republic, and then ask for admission to the American Union. On March 25, Secretary Fish, contemplating that the importance of Hawaii and the decadent tendency of the Hawaiian Government might force the United States to consider its future, instructed the United States minister to secure full and accurate information upon the population, industries, resources and debt of Hawaii, and learn the views of the Hawaiian authorities concerning the policy, manner, terms, and conditions of annexation. Regarding the American policy, he said: " While there are . . . many and influential persons in this country who question the policy of any insular acquisitions, perhaps even of any extension of territorial limits, there are also those of influence and of wise foresight who see a future that must extend the jurisdiction and the limits of this nation, and that will require a resting spot in mid-ocean, between the Pacific coast and the vast domains of Asia which are now opening to commerce and Christian civilization." Concerning the reported strong friendly sentiments in Hawaii, he said: " You will, without committing the Government to any line of policy, not discourage the feeling in favor of annexation."

Major-General Schofield, of the United States Army, had already been instructed in June, 1872, to examine the defensive capabilities and commercial facilities of Hawaiian ports. In a report to the Secretary of War (May 8, 1873), he stated that while the government and people of these islands were probably not then prepared to consider the question of annexation, even if the United States desired to propose it, they favored the cession of Pearl river harbor as a means of securing a reciprocity treaty.

Kalakaua, whom the legislative assembly chose as king at the death of Lunalilo[22] in February, 1874, showed a disposition to favor the American influence in the islands. During the riots that followed his election, he requested that an armed forced be landed from American vessels to preserve order. In 1875 he visited the United States, and his government negotiated a treaty of reciprocity which granted certain exclusive privileges to the United States, and was, for several years, the source of protests by Great Britain.

The relation of the islands to the United States and the North Pacific caused the American Government to seek an American solution for Hawaiian problems. In 1881, Secretary Blaine, in his instructions to Minister Comly, said that the gradual and seemingly inevitable decadence of the native race might induce the United States to change her policy of commercial assimilation to one of colonization and material annexation; and he desired Hawaii to coop-

---

[22] Lunalilo had succeeded Kamehameha V. whose line ended in 1872.

erate in replenishing her vital forces by the passage of favorable homestead laws that would encourage the enterprising Americans to emigrate to the islands. Secretary Frelinghuysen, though he did not consider it any part of the American policy to interpose to prevent the annexation of the outlying archipelagoes and islands of Polynesia[28] by foreign powers to whose colonial system they were geographically allied, said (1883) the United States " could not view with complacency any movement tending to the extinction of the national life of the intimately connected commonwealths of the Northern Pacific."

Secretary Bayard's policy was to prolong the reciprocity treaty and quietly wait until American planters and industries flowing to the islands should prepare for a " perfectly feasible policy of acquisition." By a convention concluded in 1884 and ratified in 1887, reciprocity was renewed for seven years, and the United States was given exclusive right to enter Pearl harbor, in Oahu, and to establish a coaling station there. Though the grant of the harbor did not impair the political sovereignty of Hawaii, it induced the British to propose that a tripartite arrangement between the United States, Great Britain and Germany should guarantee the neutrality of the islands. Bayard, seeing no necessity for joining in such an arrangement, replied that one of the articles of the reciprocity treaty inhibited a cession of any part of Hawaiian territory without consent of the American Government.

The possibility of a crisis under which it would be the policy of the United States to take possession by military occupation had been contemplated for years. In February, 1874, Minister Pierce recommended that a United States vessel should be stationed at Hawaii at all times. In May,

---

[28] In October, 1883, there was some agitation in Australia in favor of protection and eventual occupation of the New Hebrides, the Solomon, and other adjacent groups. The Hawaiian Government issued a protest, and attempted to secure the cooperation of the United States Government.

1889, his successor, G. W. Merrill, suggested that in view of the large American interests, the absence of cable communication, and the approach of a political campaign, the United States should keep a vessel in Hawaiian waters. In accordance with this suggestion, the *Adams* was soon ordered to Honolulu. The wisdom of such a policy was proven by subsequent events. On July 30, a band of natives, desiring a larger share of official patronage, and believing that foreign residents and cabinet officials were endeavoring to influence political affairs so as to destroy Hawaiian autonomy,[24] made an unsuccessful attempt at revolution. By permission of the native government, about seventy marines were landed to protect property and influence the restoration of order. Many American residents hoped that revolutionary attempts and frequent turmoils would hasten annexation.

The danger of further disturbance was increased by the election of February, 1890, which indicated a reaction from the reform constitution established by the bloodless revolution of 1787. The opposition, aided by the king, who hoped to recover part of his former autocratic power, gained votes by appealing to race prejudices and succeeded in electing many who were not friendly to the United States. Minister Stevens, expecting factional disturbance, recommended that the United States should order a war vessel to remain at Honolulu, and soon urged the establishment of a coal depot.

The dissatisfaction growing out of the change of rulers in 1891 increased annexation sentiment in Hawaii. King Kalakaua, who died in January, was succeeded by his sister, Liliuokalani, widow of an American resident, who caused much discontent by her attitude toward the legislature, and her subjection to Marshal Wilson, a half-caste Tahitian.

---

[24] The general celebration of the Fourth of July, at Honolulu, as described by Minister Merrill in a despatch of July, indicates that there was a strong American sentiment there.

On February 8, 1892, Stevens considered that annexation was the only remedy to relieve the feverish political situation and prevent the danger of England obtaining a hold a month later. Expecting a revolution against the queen's government, he intimated that the continued presence of a United States ship-of-war was necessary, and in view of possible contingencies, asked for instructions as to duties of himself and naval commanders. During the summer, naval commanders reported that conditions in Hawaii, notwithstanding the influence of the British element, seemed " to point toward an eventual request for annexation."

On November 20, in a confidential report of the financial, agricultural, social and political conditions, and the commercial and naval importance of the islands, Stevens referred to the strong inclination of Europeans to gain possession of islands in the Pacific, and stated that Hawaii was at the parting of the ways and must either become Asiatic or American—either like Singapore or Southern California. He declared that in order to subserve American commercial and political interests it was absolutely necessary either to adopt a vigorous policy of annexation or to secure cable connections with at least an implied American protectorate over the islands.

On January 15, 1893, Queen Liliuokalani attempted to promulgate a new constitution, giving herself more power, depriving foreigners of right of franchise, abrogating the House of Nobles and giving the queen power to appoint a new House. Foreigners and others strenuously opposed, and a peaceful revolution resulted in the deposition of the queen. By request of the unopposed *de facto* government, marines from the *Boston* were landed to preserve order,[25] and Minister Stevens, on February 1, assumed protection of the island. Secretary J. W. Foster commended his action so far as it accorded protection to life and property, but disavowed it so far as it might appear to overstep

[25] Lucian Young: The *Boston* at Hawaii, Washington, 1898.

that limit by setting the authority and power of the United States above that of the government of the Hawaiian Islands in the capacity of a protector, or impair in any way the sovereignty of the Hawaiian Government.[26]

The provisional government, which was recognized by Minister Stevens and all foreign governments except England, had already sent commissioners to Washington and negotiated a treaty of annexation, which President Harrison, on February 15, sent to the United States Senate for confirmation. While the treaty was yet pending in the Senate, President Cleveland was inaugurated, and ex-Queen Liliuokalani, having complained that the recent " revolt " had been aided by United States troops, he soon recalled the treaty from the Senate and ordered an investigation of the revolution.[27] On April 14, 1893, awaiting action by Congress, President Cleveland withdrew the protectorate established by Stevens on February 9.

Refusing to reinstate the queen, the leaders in Hawaii on July 4, 1894, dissolved the provisional government and proclaimed a republic. A movement for annexation was vigorously pushed, and on June 16, 1897, a treaty of annexation was sent to the Senate by President McKinley. The Senate did not act, but after the opening of the war with Spain, a joint resolution in favor of annexation was passed by Congress and was signed by President McKinley on July 7, 1898, soon after the occupation of Manila, where the American flag now floated over the fortifications of the Philippines.

NOTES ON HAWAIIAN CONSTITUTIONAL HISTORY.— American influence is seen in Hawaiian constitutional development.

---

[26] For political correspondence, 1889-93, see H. Exec. Doc. 48, 53-2, Dec. 18, 1893. [Reprint of Sen. Exec. Docs. 76 and 77, 52-2, Feb., 1893.]

[27] Commissioner Blount's report is in H. Exec. Doc. 47, 53-2, Dec. 18, 1893. Also, see Sen. Rp. 227, 53-2, Feb. 26, 1894 [773 pp. and maps], and Foreign Relations, 1894, Appendix ii.

In 1839, American missionaries and ex-missionaries persuaded Kamehameha III. to sign a Bill of Rights, and in October, 1840, they induced him to grant a constitution, giving up his absolute power, providing for four departments of administration, and creating a single legislative body composed of hereditary nobles and seven representatives formally elected by the people. This constitution, Mosaic in character, showing derivation from the Pentateuch, the British Government and the American Declaration of Independence, lasted for twelve years. By 1851 the majority of the representatives, executive officials and judges were natives of the United States.[28]

In 1852, the Government agreed upon a revised and much more liberal constitution, which existed until August, 1864. It still contained some of the levitical elements, and opened with " God hath created all men free and equal." It divided the legislative assembly into two houses, both of which were enlarged; provided for manhood suffrage and elections by ballot; denied political rights to any who should import slaves; and established a Kuhina-nui to regulate the government machine and counsel and restrict the king. The Kuhina-nui was usually a woman. She and the king each had a negative upon the other's acts. She had charge of the Great Seal, the royal standard and the national flag, and performed the duties of the king at the latter's death.[29]

In November, 1863, Kamehameha IV., who had reigned since 1854, died, and was succeeded by his brother, Prince Lot, who ruled until 1872, as Kamehameha V. The new king, showing a tendency toward the former royal absolutism, was opposed to part of the constitution of 1852, and refused to take the oath which it prescribed.[30] Seeking the

---

[28] In 1850, the king recommended a new constitution and appointed a committee of three to frame a model. Dr. Judd was the leading member.

[29] Eclectic M., Apr. 1865.

[30] His cabinet consisted of a Scotchman, an Englishman, a Frenchman and an American.

quickest way to amend the constitution so as to abolish universal suffrage and place voting upon an income and property basis, he called a convention, which was opened in July, 1864. This convention, of which the king was president, consisted of twenty-seven delegates and sixteen nobles headed by the Kuhina-nui. Mr. Judd, who was made secretary, appointed Anglo-Saxons to fill the positions of chaplain, reporter, etc. Many American missionaries, fearing that the king desired to assume extra powers, had raised the cry of alarm. When the convention met, the American party led by Dr. Judd (the ex-minister) and his son (the secretary) and three or four others, stood for manhood suffrage, and opposed the policy of the king, whose views, delivered in both English and Hawaiian, were seconded by most of the nobles.

There were some remarkable speeches. Honorable D. Kalana and others, pointing to the United States for illustration, urged that universal suffrage led to corruption at the polls, and insisted that it was not the purpose of the king to take away the poor people's rights. M. Varigny, on the part of the king, intimated that to give suffrage to the poor was like placing a razor in the hands of a baby or giving a candle into the hands of a man to carry into a powder magazine. The opposition, denying that poverty was any argument against suffrage, urged that the ballot was an incentive to work, and claimed that purity of elections existed in the United States.

After a week of debates, a decision was reached that all three estates should sit in debate in the same chamber and vote unitedly on rules or by-laws, but that constitutional subjects must first be offered and carried by the representatives (lower house), then receive the separate vote of the nobles and the sanction of the king. The opposition of the representatives caused business to move slowly, and the king, becoming impatient on account of the long discussions on " Article 62," and the failure to agree, after five weeks of fretful inculcation, declared it useless to prolong the session, and claimed the right to abrogate the constitution of 1852. " I will give you a constitution," said he, and dissolved the convention.

On August 20 the promised constitution appeared. It omitted the " free and equal " clause; reversed the bicameral arrangement and returned to the single legislative chamber; abolished the Kuhina-nui; gave the king a larger place in the state; made the cabinet more responsible; excluded the ballot; required that representatives should own real estate worth $500, or have an annual income of $250, and that electors, besides possessing certain intellectual requirements, should own property worth $150, or receive $25 yearly rent and leasehold and $75 income. This constitution existed until 1887, when the legislative powers of the crown became entirely vested in the representatives of the people. The attempt of Liliuokalani in June, 1893, to increase her power and deprive foreigners of the right of suffrage by a new constitution resulted in the revolution that made Hawaii a republic, and prepared the way for annexation to the United States. The present territorial government was established by act of Congress in 1900.[1]

---

[1] See appendix.

CHAPTER IX.

RELATIONS IN SAMOA.

The attitude of the United States toward the Samoan Islands furnishes an instructive chapter in the evolution of national policy. Compared to its policy in Hawaii, the American Government until recently has shown little interest in securing a control over the islands in the South Pacific, but local conditions, together with the increase of American interests in the Pacific and the Far East, led us first to a policy of protection for Samoa,[1] and then to division and acquisition.

---

[1] The Samoan Islands, located 4200 miles southwest from San Francisco, and 420 miles northeast of the Fijis, discovered in 1772 by a Hollander, are the largest and most populous Pacific group, with the exception of the Hawaiian Islands. Of the 13 islands in the group, only Savaii (700 square miles), Upolo (550 square miles), and Tutuila (55 square miles) are inhabited. The others are little more than barren volcanic rocks. The population is about 30,000, and the area about equal to that of Rhode Island. There are about 300 Europeans and Americans on the islands. The climate is tropical, and frequent thunder showers throughout the year supply the necessary irrigation for the rank vegetation. The products are bread-fruit, taro, yams, bananas, sugar, coffee, sea-island cotton, cocoanuts, etc. The lagoons and reefs abound in fish, which the natives catch with spears and nets. Both the import and export trade is in the hands of Germans. All accounts are kept in terms of United States currency. The natives are hospitable, open, amiable, brave and hardy and possess great mental ability, but are averse to labor. They speak a language similar to that of the Hawaiians. The principal amusements are quoits, card playing (casino), cricket and the *siva*, a kind of acting charade in which the life of the islands is represented in a very realistic manner by " living pictures." The actual *siva* is performed by girls, smeared with cocoa-nut oil, who frequently, under the excitement of their motions and contortions, divest themselves of all clothing. The marriage ceremony is very simple, and often there is no ceremony except the mere expression of a willingness to live together.

It was seen that the position of the islands, on the great trade routes between Panama and California, on the one hand, and Australia and the Orient, on the other, together with their strategic advantages, both political and commercial, were more important than the value of their trade. The harbor of Pango Pango (on the Tutuila), which is owned by the United States, is the best place in the South Pacific for repair and supplies and for a coaling and cable station. The harbor of Apia, under German control, though a safe port under ordinary conditions, has proven unsatisfactory in a severe storm.

Though an American consul had resided at Apia many years before [2] to protect American interests, our closer relations began in 1872, when Commander R. W. Meade, a United States navy officer, of the *Narragansett*,[3] on his own responsibility, entered into an agreement pledging the protection of the United States, stating that we were about to establish commercial relations with the islands by means of a line of steamers then plying between California, Hawaii, New Zealand and Australia, and desired a convenient coaling port.

Both parties to a dormant civil war, which had been pending in Samoa since 1870, interfering with the exports of the island and causing the natives to spend most of the time in sharpening their war knives and axes, expressed a wish to acknowledge the absolute authority of the United

---

Polygamy has almost ceased. In case of divorce the young children go to the mother. Cooking is done by the men, and each person at the meal uses a bread-fruit leaf for a table, a mat for a chair, and the nearest post for a table napkin. The early social, political, and religious life of the Samoans is an interesting study. See George Turner's " Samoa a hundred years ago and long before," [Macmillan, 1884], and J. B. Stair's " Old Samoa," [London, 1897]. A good review of Turner's volume appears in the Nation [N. Y.] of August 21, 1884.

[2] See Senate Rp. Com. 148, 36-1.

[3] Geo. B. Rieman: Narrative of a cruise of the U. S. Str. *Narragansett*, Oakland, Cal., 1874, 43 pp. Nineteenth Century, Feb., 1886.

States, and on March 2 the Chief of Pango Pango " freely and voluntarily " signed a treaty with Commander Meade, granting the United States the exclusive privilege of establishing a naval and coal depot in the bay in return for the promise of friendly alliance and protection by the United States.[4] In May, Grant, stating that he would not hesitate to recommend its approval, but for the protection to which it seemed to pledge the United States, sent the treaty to the Senate,[5] which failed to ratify it.

In 1873 the Department of State determined to obtain further information regarding the condition of Samoa. Colonel A. B. Steinberger, sent for this purpose, reached the islands in 1874. Under him the chiefs assembled a council, formed a constitution and laws for a united government, and again asked Grant to take the country under the protection of the United States. Steinberger, after making a voluminous report[6] on the fertility and resources and important position of the islands, was impatient to return, and the Government again sent him with the condition that he pay his own expenses. He received instructions, dated December 11, in which Secretary Fish doubted whether the importance of a commanding position in the Pacific was a sufficient consideration to satisfy the people that the annexation of the islands was essential to our safety and prosperity, and did not consider it expedient " to originate a measure adverse to the usual tradition of the Government."

---

[4] The treaty also provided for the protection of the persons and property of foreigners and foreign consuls, the regulation of port charges and pilotage, the prohibition of trade in intoxicating liquors and work on Sunday, the apprehension of deserters, and of foreigners from encouraging native females to prostitute themselves.

[5] On March 16, 1872, President Grant, in response to a House resolution, sent a reply of the Secretary of State of same date, stating that there were no papers in the Department of State to show that the inhabitants of the Navigators' Islands, in the Pacific had made any application to have the protection of the United States extended over said islands.

[6] Sen. Exec. Doc. 45, 43-1, Apr. 22, 1874.

Returning to Samoa in 1875, he, Steinberger, dethroned Tupua, made Malietoa sole king, changed the constitution, made himself prime minister of a new government which he established in the financial interest of a German (Hamburg) mercantile firm, and gave the impression that the islands were under the protection of the United States, but the American Government refused to support him. Embarrassed by the renewal of the turbulent spirit among the chiefs, he fell into trouble as a ruler, and being unable to produce any credentials from Washington, was deported with the concurrence of the American consul. A new government, organized under a council of chiefs, continued till May, 1879, when, by the decision of the consular representatives of the United States, Great Britain and Germany, Malietoa was recognized and anointed as king. Steinberger's action had been upon his own responsibility, and without the authority of the United States Government. The purpose of his mission and the character of the power conferred upon him were the subject of inquiry by the House. The President responded on May 1, communicating copies of the correspondence, showing that the United States was not implicated.[7] An instruction to Steinberger, written after the report that he had promised the Samoans the protection of the United States, regretted his action, stating that the United States Government had not held out any hope of such protection, and that the State Department, without a treaty or sanction of Congress, had no right to authorize such a promise.

In both 1877 and 1878 consular representatives of the United States at Apia, " disregarding our traditional policy," raised the United States flag as sign of a protectorate, but the United States Government did not sustain their acts.

In 1877, one of the Samoan parties,[8] seeking repose from

---

[7] H. Exec. Doc. 161, 44-1, May 1, 1876. H. Exec. Doc. 44, 44-2, March 2, 1877. The correspondence may be seen in Sen. Exec. Doc. 97, 53-3, vol. vi, Feb. 26, 1895.

[8] At the same time, another party sent its chiefs to Fiji to solicit British protection.

war, and doubtful of their ability to maintain peace and independence, sent Mamea as ambassador to Washington to seek American protection; but Secretary Evarts, though he wished to see a " stable, independent government " that would command the respect of nations and foreigners and end the schemes of disorder, was not willing to accept a protectorate over islands so far distant. In 1878, however, the United States finally concluded a treaty, receiving Pango Pango as a coaling station and agreeing to mediate for the adjustment of difficulties in which Samoa might become involved with a European power.[9] Soon thereafter, Germany also made a treaty by which she secured a naval station in the harbor of Saluafata, and Great Britain negotiated a treaty granting her a naval and coaling station.

In 1879 the foreign powers induced the natives to make a peace agreement by which one party supplied the king and the other the vice-king, both of whom were to preside over a government of lords and commons supposed to be elective. But the elective system existed only in name. Samoans did not trouble themselves about their franchise, and soon the chiefs ignored the whole system and themselves decided who should be representatives. They appeared incapable of carrying on a stable government. Their government had no funds and no system of taxation. They had a parliament without a general parliament house. Discussion was carried on from house to house, each political division having a house. There was oratory, much squabbling, scheming and procrastination, but no voting. If the opposition felt strong enough it would leave and go home to prepare to fight.[10]

The Samoan government was a bone of contention between the foreign consuls. In 1880[11] a scheme of tripartite

[9] On the reception of the treaty and the political situation at Samoa, see Sen. Exec. Doc. 2, 46-1. Mar. 21, 1879.

[10] W. B. Churchward: My Consulate in Samoa [1881-85], London, 1887.

[11] About the same time the United States saw the need of extending the jurisdiction of her Apia consuls to outlying islands, and

local government by the consular representatives of the United States, Great Britain and Germany was proposed, but the United States did not consider the plan desirable. The Samoans themselves were becoming tired of a shuttlecock existence. In 1884, Malietoa and the vice-king begged Queen Victoria to either make Samoa a British colony or allow it to be governed by New Zealand.

German residents, acquiring land and monopolizing trade, had continued to encourage opposition to the king, and in 1884 the German consul precipitated a crisis by securing from the Samoan council an agreement providing for a German-Samoan council of government. The king, refusing to execute the agreement, Steubel, the German consul, in 1885, raised his flag over Apia and took possession in the name of his Government as security for Samoan good behavior toward German interests. The American consul, Greenbaum, to counteract German influence, proceeded to hoist the American flag and proclaim a protectorate. The United States Government disavowed the action of Greenbaum, but spoke in a determined tone regarding the protection of American rights in the Pacific.[12]

In the early part of 1886, the State Department was informed that Germany, having agreed with England upon lines of Pacific division,[13] claimed sovereignty over Samoa, and the hitherto unclaimed Gilbert and Marshall islands in which, as in other outlying, unattached groups, the representatives of many nationalities had sporadically settled.

---

was ready to aid native and independent government of the Ralick groups of Marshall archipelago in establishing temperance restrictions.

[12] Bayard to Pendleton, Jan. 17, 1888.

[13] In 1885, both Spain and Germany claimed the Caroline Islands, where large American interests were already established. Germany seemed to suspect the intention of the United States to assert a claim to the islands, but Secretary Bayard announced our purpose to respect whatever sovereign jurisdiction might be established or already exist there, without indicating an opinion on the Spanish-German controversy.

The United States had no treaty relations with either the Gilbert or Marshall groups, and offered no objection to their annexation by Germany, but insisted that interests created in favor of peaceful American settlers there should not be disturbed by any assertion of exclusive claims of territorial jurisdiction. In some cases American citizens had undisturbed possession of the Pacific islands, and the United States could have asserted a claim of possession, but she did not desire any exclusive jurisdiction for herself and was not ready to allow any jurisdiction by others if it should expel American citizens from rights which they had from the natives.[14]

Determining to get authentic information regarding the situation in Samoa, Bayard sent (1886) George H. Bates, his law partner, to investigate and to prepare an exhaustive report.[15] Desiring to extend good offices for the establishment of order in Samoa, he suggested a conference of representatives of the three powers which, in June, 1887, met at Washington to negotiate a treaty securing autonomy and neutrality of the islands. He urged that the "autonomy and independence of Samoa should be scrupulously preserved," a principle upon which President Cleveland had insisted in a special message to Congress in the preceding January. He proposed that each treaty power should alternately keep a man-of-war in Samoan waters four months

---

[14] The interest of the United States in regard to the destiny of the Pacific islands was increased by the rapid absorption of various groups by the European powers. Great Britain, who had appropriated Australia a century earlier, accepted the Fijis in 1874. France, who had taken the Marquesas, in 1842, and the New Caledonian and Loyalty islands, in 1853, extended her control to the Society group, in 1880; Spain, who had occupied the Philippines and Ladrones since the sixteenth century, took possession of the Carolines, in 1885; Germany assumed control of the Marshall, Solomon and Admiralty groups; Holland and Germany partitioned New Guinea. In 1888, Great Britain took Gilbert, Ellice, Union and Enderbury groups, and several single islands, including Fanning, Washington, Starbuck and Caroline.

[15] Strictly Confidential Report of G. H. Bates to the Secretary of State, Dec. 10, 1886. Washington, 1887, 135 pp.

of each year to aid in maintaining the government to be established and to preserve peace and order. He also proposed that administration of laws be, by an executive council, composed of the king, vice-king and three foreigners, one of whom should be designated by each of the foreign powers, but all of whom should be [16] paid by the Samoan Government. The plan which Germany desired, and the British seemed to favor, committing the practical control of affairs to a German adviser of the king, he feared would give Germany too much influence in the Samoan Government. Failing to agree upon any plan, the conference adjourned in July.

The Germans in Samoa, by mortgages and land sales, were rapidly getting possession of territory which the natives had never intended to sell,[17] and appeared to be preparing to seize the islands. From the government of Malietoa, hampered by a House of Lords and a House of Commons that did as they pleased, and attempting to rule over a people who refused to obey its orders, they expected little protection for white settlers. By defeating Malietoa and setting up another king with a German adviser, they precipitated a civil contest in which the Samoans were divided into two hostile camps of armed warriors,[18] one supported by German arms, and the other by British colonels and citizens of the United States; they declared martial law at Apia and tried to enforce it on Americans, who at once registered a strong protest.[19]

---

[16] . . . Blaine, on April 11, 1889, in instructions to our negotiators at the Berlin conference, said that the plan proposed by the United States, in the conference of 1887, was hardly less than a joint protectorate; it went beyond the principle upon which President Harrison desired to see our Samoan relations based, was not in harmony with our established policy, and did not promise efficient action.

[17] In 1886, they claimed 232,000 acres, and the British subjects 357,000 acres.

[18] See an article by Henry C. Ide in N. Am. Rev., Aug., 1897.

[19] Commander Leary of the U. S. warship *Adams* on Sept. 6, 1888, sent a protest to the captain of one of the German vessels. Marines were landed to protect the American consulate.

The United States, though she had not consciously sought to participate in the contest, and though her trade with Samoa was small compared with that of Germany and England, threatened intervention in order to preserve her interests in the Pacific.[20] She promptly sent a naval squadron, which was subsequently destroyed in the hurricane of 1889.[21] Congress, after an examination of reports and much discussion, appropriated $500,000 for protective measures. On January 17, 1888, in a letter to Pendleton, replying to Bismarck's complaints as to the anti-German attitude of Sewall, the American consul at Apia, Secretary Bayard, reviewing the absorption of Pacific islands by European powers since 1840, and especially since 1884, was determined that only the American Government should preserve Samoan independence and maintain the rights to which the United States had become entitled in any of the few remaining islands which were still under independent and autonomous governments.[22]

In February, 1889, Bayard gladly accepted Bismarck's proposal for a resumption of the joint conference for a tripartite agreement. President Harrison appointed John A. Kasson, William Walter Phelps and George H. Bates as plenipotentiaries to go to Berlin. A convention,[23] concluded the following June, provided for maintaining the neutrality of the islands and stipulated that the three powers should refrain from exercising any separate control over the islands or the government. It contained clauses prohibiting the sale of intoxicating liquors, establishing a system of registering titles, and securing to American citizens equality with others in trade, etc.

---

[20] H. Exec. Doc. vol. viii, No. 1, 51-1.

[21] R. L. Stevenson: In South Seas, 1888-89. N. Y., 1896.

[22] On American rights in Samoa, see H. Exec. Doc. 238, 50-1, Apr. 2, 1888, 311 pp. For the condition of Samoan affairs, see Sen. Exec. Docs. 31, 68 and 118, 50-2, Dec. 1888 and Jan. 1889. Also, a pamphlet of 77 pages, " Confidential correspondence respecting affairs in Samoa " [December, 1888-March, 1889], printed for the use of the American Commissioners to Berlin in 1889.

[23] S. Misc. Doc. 81, 51-1, Jan. 6, 1890.

The principal features of the government as provided by the treaty were as follows:

(1) A single king, chosen by the chiefs, a salary of $1800, instead of the two rival kings, who had received $500 each;

(2) A supreme court with a chief justice nominated by the three foreign powers (or by the King of Sweden in case of disagreement), with a salary of $6000 guaranteed by the powers. (The clerk and marshal were to be paid by fees.) The chief justice was given jurisdiction of all Samoan questions arising under the treaty, between the treaty powers, and as to the election of king, and could recommend the passage of laws. He had exclusive jurisdiction in suits between natives and foreigners, or between foreigners of different nationalities, and of crimes and offences committed by natives against foreigners.

(3) A local government for the district of Apia (170 electors), consisting of a municipal council of six members and a president. The president, who was also chief executive of the district and adviser to the king, was appointed through the instrumentality of treaty powers, who guaranteed him $5000 per year out of the Samoan revenues assigned to the municipality. The municipal council appointed a municipal magistrate and subordinate officers, but its orders had no effect till approved by the three foreign consuls or (if they failed to agree) by the chief justice.

(4) A land commission of three persons, one named by each power, for examination of claims and titles, subject to final jurisdiction of the chief justice. (Each commissioner received $300 per month and expenses.)

(5) A fiscal system, providing for revenue duties on imports and exports, capitation taxes on Samoans and colored plantation laborers, license taxes, etc. All taxes collected at Apia were to belong to the municipality, and those collected elsewhere were to belong to the Samoan Government.[24]

---

[24] In the condition of affairs in the islands this provision resulted in leaving the government without adequate means of sup-

Though the Samoan Government accepted the treaty, and the chiefs elected Malietoa king, the rebellious symptoms of the opposition party gradually increased. The natives remaining inveterately opposed to a centralized or civilized government, refused to pay capitation taxes or to obey warrants of the supreme court, which opened its doors in June, 1891. Mataafa and his turbulent followers continued (1891) to gather strength and to live in open defiance of the king and government, keeping up an armed force, plundering foreigners and plantations, and harboring refugees from justice.[25] In July, 1893, war broke out and the treaty powers actively intervened with naval forces to keep Malietoa on the throne, and soon deported eleven chiefs to another island, where they were kept at the joint expense of the three powers. Meanwhile the chief justice and the president of the municipal council of Apia resigned. In November, 1893, H. C. Ide, an American member of the land commission, was appointed chief justice, but he found the laws silent and insurrection constantly threatening. Though the king succeeded in repelling his opponents in battle, he requested that foreign war-vessels preserve peace and security (1894).

Though both Bayard and Bates had contemplated the necessity of assistance from the powers to maintain the government established by the treaty,[26] and Gresham, as late as June, 1893, had informed Pauncefote that the United States Government would "join in an active demonstration against Mataafa," President Cleveland sent no

---

port and became a subject of concern and discussion among the three powers, who were compelled to continue their pecuniary support of the government.

[25] In January, 1893, many in the United States Senate thought we had made a mistake in refusing to accept annexation or extend a protectorate when the opportunity was offered.

[26] On February 20, 1893, Blaine, in a letter to Pauncefote, also stated that in the execution of the spirit of the treaty of Berlin the treaty powers should send war vessels to sustain the Samoan authorities and enforce the warrants of the supreme court by proper and judicious means.

war vessels, and considering the islands commercially worthless and the inhabitants intractable, in his messages of 1893,
1894 and 1895, recommended withdrawal from the treaty.[27]
Though the treaty of 1889 had been a deliberate act of national policy in our international relations, both Cleveland
and Secretary Gresham urged that it was a mistake, expensive, annoying and involving us in entangling alliances.[28]

Gresham referred to the Samoan government as in sub-
stance and form a tripartite foreign government imposed
upon the natives, and supported and administered jointly
by the three treaty powers.   On May 9, 1894, a report to
President Cleveland said: "It is in our relations with
Samoa that we have made the first departure from our traditional and well-established policy of avoiding entangling
alliances with foreign powers in relation to objects remote
from this hemisphere.   Like all other human transactions,
the wisdom of that departure must be tested by its fruits.
. . . Every nation, and especially every strong nation, must
sometimes be conscious of an impulse to rush into difficulties that do not concern it, except in a highly imaginary
way.   To restrain the indulgence of such a propensity is
not only the part of wisdom, but a duty we owe to the
world as an example of the strength, the moderation and
the beneficence of popular government. . . . The whole
trade of the islands is of small value, and of this only a small
part is with the United States.   We have never found it
wise to interfere in the affairs of a foreign country in order
to trade with it." [29]

---

[27] See an article by H. C. Ides in the N. Am. Rev. for Aug., 1897.

[28] The *Nation* said the result of the treaty arranged was con-
tinual unrest, disturbance and foreign interference and opposed the
modern mania for foreign dependencies at great distances from
our shores, stating that if Samoa belonged to any system it belonged to the Australian system, and that the New Zealanders,
had more reason than the United States to complain of German
meddling.   [Nation, May 17, 1894.]

[29] For Gresham's review of American relations as to Samoa, see
"Foreign Relations," 1894, Appendix i, pp. 504-13.   Also, Senate
Exec. Doc. 93, 53-2, vol. iv.

The long-range government of refractory, indocile natives, with all its perplexities, under the international joint
protectorate continued to be unsatisfactory and expensive,
but no better plan acceptable to all could be suggested.[30]
The death of King Malietoa Lampepa, in August, 1898,
finally produced a crisis which resulted in a new arrangement. The election of a successor developed a contest as
to the validity of the result, and rival claimants took the
field. Chief Justice Chambers (from Alabama) with his
great power, acting by the terms of the general act, rendered his judgment in favor of Malietoa Tanu, and
Mataafa, encouraged by the German consul, and with more
followers than the king had, took up arms. Marines from
American and British warships intervened to restore order.[31]

Steps were taken to improve relations between the United
States and Germany, and to avoid any occasion for further
friction in Samoa,[32] a joint commission of representatives of
the United States, Great Britain and Germany were sent to
investigate affairs at Samoa, and to propose a remedy. It
soon abolished the kingship and established a provisional
government. The partition of the islands, as Blaine had
planned in 1889, or annexation of the whole group by a
single power, appeared to offer best promise of a satisfactory
permanent settlement.

---

[30] Foreign Relations, 1896, pp. 531-54; also, 1895, pp. 1126-59.

[31] *The Nation,* Jan. 26, 1899.

[32] William Blacklock, the United States vice-consul-general, who
advocated annexation as the only permanent settlement, in a statement of his views for the commission in June, 1899, said:

"The mode of dealing with the natives from the beginning by
the powers interested in Samoa has been calculated to make the
Samoan a most important individual in his own estimation. Stacks
of proclamations have been posted and endless orders from warships been issued, but none has ever been thoroughly enforced,
and the consequence is that now the natives ignore proclamations and laugh at threats of men-of-war. They imagine themselves unconquerable, even by the three powers combined, and
every time there is an outbreak they go a little further than the
time before."

The United States was determined not to abandon her interests to Germany and England. The latter, however, agreed to retire, in view of compensation by Germany in other directions, and in a treaty providing for a discontinuance by the joint protectorate both powers renounced (November, 1894), in favor of the United States, all their rights and claims to that portion of the group east of 171 west longitude, including Tutuila and other smaller islands. By the same convention the United States agreed to renounce all claims to the islands of the group lying west of 171, thus giving the Germans the preponderating force which they had exercised in that region before the treaty of Berlin was made. She received a guarantee, however, for the same privileges and conditions as those possessed by Germany in respect to commerce and commercial vessels in all the islands of Samoa. Malietoa, after an unsuccessful protest, expressed his views in a letter to the London Times, in which he took occasion to assert that the civilization introduced by the great powers in their annexations in the islands of the South Seas is inferior to the primitive state of those islands.[33]

The American flag now floats over the naval station at Pango Pango, and the island of Tutuila is under the control of the navy, but there has been no interference with the political self-government of the natives, who have appeared delighted to pass under the sovereignty and protection of the United States.

---

[33] London Times, January 12, 1900.

CHAPTER X.

OCCUPATION OF THE PHILIPPINES.

The Philippines, which have recently and unexpectedly enlarged the sphere of the United States in the Far East, were visited by Americans at a very early date in our national history. After the close of the war of 1812, Secretary Monroe took steps to obtain information regarding conditions there and to secure a report on the prospects for trade. In March, 1817, Andrew Stuart, who had resided in Manila since 1812, received from President Madison a commission as United States consul at that place. For several years he was not officially recognized by the Spanish authorities, but he was allowed to remain and was not obstructed in the performance of the duties of a consul.[1] In September, 1818, he reported that the Spanish authorities had found several Americans among the crew of the *Argentina*, a Buenos Ayres privateer, which had been obstructing the provincial commerce for several months. Writing to Secretary Adams, in June, 1819, he stated that unless interrupted by the "proverbially suspicious government," he proposed to place the United States in possession of Royal nautical directions for the guidance of galleons and for the harbors to which they resorted, together with charts and drawings showing "tracks laid down in unpublished Spanish plans," which he suggested might "assume an aspect of great national and political importance and utility . . . should the amicable relations between the two governments ever be interrupted or ruptured."

About the same time, Lieutenant John White, of the

---

[1] Consular Letters, Manila, vol. i, 1817-40. [MS.]

United States navy, after arriving at Cavite and Manila, and taking breakfast with Stuart, wrote: " The spirit of independence which has recently diffused its influence through Spanish colonies on the American continent has also darted its rays across the Pacific . . . and the time is perhaps not very remote when it shall burst forth and shed its joyous light upon the remotest and most inconsiderable islet of this archipelago." . . . " Perhaps no part of the world offers a more eligible site for an independent republic than these islands." [2]

In November, 1820, Consul Stuart, writing of recent native maraudings, murders and riots, and feeling that the Government was too slow in declaring martial law, suggesting that the recently published new constitution was too liberal to the natives and expecting a general revolution to result, said the Filipinos were treacherous, ungrateful and " insensible of any favor done them," and " ought to be governed rather strict(ly) to keep them obedient to the laws, make them industrious, to work in every mode against their natural and old inclinations." [3]   At that time there was little demand for American goods, but by 1834, Consul H. W. Edwards, noticing the increase of imports of American manufacturing goods, said: " These islands will eventually be the outlet of our manufactures to a great extent."

The United States, though she annexed the Philippines as a result of long-evolving circumstances,[4] acquired them as the result of no long-contemplated plans.   In 1898, at the beginning of the war of intervention in Cuba, she had "no design of aggrandizement and no ambition of conquest." Needing a naval station and a port where our war vessels could find protection and desiring to reduce the strength of the enemy, after the declaration of war, the American Government ordered Dewey to destroy the Spanish fleet at

---

[2] John White: A Voyage to the China Sea. Boston, 1823.
[3] Consular Letters, Manila, vol. i, 1817-40.
[4] R. H. Bancroft: The New Pacific.

Manila. By a brave dash into the harbor, we soon held the key to the Philippines and cut off communication with Madrid. To hasten peace we sent an army of occupation across the Pacific. At the close of the war, though we had taken up arms " without any original thought of complete or even partial acquisition," the presence and success of our arms in Manila brought our republican empire new opportunities which she could not wisely reject, and new duties and responsibilities which she could not courageously and honorably avoid. Having obtained occupation of a rich prize, whose value was well known by European powers that would have seized it at first opportunity without hesitation, and seeing the value of a permanent establishment at the gates of the East, the McKinley administration in the peace negotiations of 1898, accepting the logic of our history, resolved to relieve Spain of insular dependencies she had only held with a weak hand and which, under American control, would have the opportunity to enjoy greater freedom, and would give the American nation a greater place in the affairs of the world.

On October 28, 1898, the American Peace Commissioners at Paris were instructed as follows: " Territorial expansion should be our least concern; that we shall not shirk the moral obligations of our victory is of the greatest. It is indisputed that Spain's authority is permanently destroyed in every part of the Philippines. To leave any part in her feeble control now would increase our difficulties and be opposed to the interests of humanity. Nor can we permit Spain to transfer any of the islands to another power. Nor can we invite another power or powers to join the United States in sovereignty over them. We must either hold them or turn them back to Spain.

" Consequently, grave as are the responsibilities and unforeseen as are the difficulties which are before us, the President can see but one plain path of duty—the acceptance of the archipelago. Greater difficulties and more serious complications, administrative and international, would follow any other course. The President has given to the view of the commissioners the fullest consideration, and in reaching the conclusion above announced in the light of information communicated to the commission and to the President since your departure, he has been influenced by the single consideration of duty and humanity. The President is not unmindful of the distressed financial condition of Spain, and whatever consideration the United States may show must come from its sense of generosity and benevolence, rather than from any real or technical obligation."

On November 13, the following additional instructions were sent:

" From the standpoint of indemnity both the archipelagoes (Porto Rico and the Philippines) are insufficient to pay our war expenses, but aside from this, do we not owe an obligation to the people of the Philippines which will not permit us to return them to the sovereignty of Spain? Could we justify ourselves in such a course or could we permit their barter to some other power? Willing or not, we have the responsibility of duty which we cannot escape. The President cannot believe any division of the archipelago can bring us anything but embarrassment in the future. The trade and commercial side, as well as the indemnity for the cost of the war, are questions we might yield. They might be waived or compromised, but the questions of duty and humanity appeal to the President so strongly that he can find no appropriate answer but the one he has here marked out."

The treaty of peace [5] of December 10 provided that Spain, beside withdrawing from the West Indies, should cede to the United States the archipelago known as the Philippine Islands; that the United States should pay to Spain the sum of $20,000,000, and that the civil rights and political status of the native inhabitants should be determined by Congress.

The treaty was ratified by the Senate on February 6, 1899,

---

[5] Sen. Doc. 62, part i, 55-3, Jan. 4, 1899, 677 pp.

and by the Government of Spain on the 19th of March following. The ratifications were exchanged on the 11th of April and the treaty publicly proclaimed. On the 2d of March Congress voted the sum contemplated by the treaty, and the amount was paid over to the Spanish Government on the 1st of May. The United States, though acting on the principle that " there must be no joint occupation with the insurgents," who were in arms against the Spanish Government in the Philippines, had from the time of American occupation assured the people that the United States Government desired to advance their interests and welfare. On the 21st of December, after the treaty was signed, the commander of the forces of occupation was instructed " to announce and proclaim in the most public manner that we come not as invaders and conquerors, but as friends to protect the natives in their homes, in their employments and in their personal and religious rights.

With a desire to establish peace and order, and as much self-government as was " compatible with the welfare of the people," in January, 1899, President McKinley sent to Manila, Commissioners Schurman, Denby and Worcester, who, in association with Admiral Dewey and Major-General Otis, were instructed " to facilitate the most humane and effective extension of authority throughout the islands and to secure with the least possible delay the benefits of a wise and generous protection of life and property to the inhabitants." Before they reached Manila, Aguinaldo, claiming that a United States officer had promised that the islands should be independent, directed the Filipinos in an attack on the American lines and precipitated a condition full of embarrassment to the United States and grievous in its consequences to the islanders.[*]

Aside from an ignominious retreat, which would have exhibited a " nerveless pusillanimity," and abandoned the islands to strife and anarchy, making them an apple of dis-

---

[*] Sen. Doc. 208, 56-1, Mar. 5, 1900, 173 pp. +

cord among rival powers, the only course remaining for the United States was to subdue the unprovoked and wasteful insurrection, preparatory to the establishment of order and the reconstruction of the government. The commissioners, in their report, said: " Our obligations to other nations and to the friendly Filipinos, and to ourselves and our flag, demanded that force should be met by force." For the restoration and maintenance of order in the Philippines, including the Sulu peninsula, the recent haunt of piracy, we were responsible to the world. To renounce the authority which we had accepted tacitly and by treaty, and give the islands an independence for which they were not prepared, would have been unjust to the loyal majority who sought American protection. To have declared the islands independent under an American protectorate, would have made us responsible for the acts of the insurgent leaders without the power to control them, and would have involved us in endless tasks of adjusting quarrels between factions in the islands and between the islands and foreign powers.[7]

Judge W. H. Taft, professedly an anti-expansionist, in a speech at Cincinnati on March 5, 1900, said:

" My conviction is that the calm investigation of the future historian into all the conditions existing at the time of taking each step toward the present situation in the Philippines will lead him to conclude that President McKinley and his Administration selected in each crisis the only alternative which a due regard to our national and international obligations would permit."

American control of the Philippines will mean the new dawn of freedom, progress and civilization to the islanders. During the declining insurrection the islands have necessarily been under military authority. President McKinley's policy has been " to inaugurate governments essentially popular in their form as fast as territory is held and controlled by our troops," beginning the work of reconstruction

---

[7] Sen. Doc. 138, 56-1, vol. i (Jan. 31, 1900), 264 pp.

by first forming municipal and provincial governments and leaving the establishment of a central government at Manila for the last step. He has sent a commission as a substitute for military government, and as a preliminary step to the establishment of a territorial form of government when it may be possible to give the natives the right of suffrage.

* *
*

The changing conditions in Asia, the mother of races, are observed with interest by the entire world. From the East to the Far East, fact is overcoming fancy, and new life takes the place of the fading, vanishing pictures of the past. Modern, relentless progressiveness is gaining a foothold in the land of Abraham, Isaac and Jacob, in the land of Moab, in the Garden of Eden, and in the homes of Confucius and Buddha. The walls of Jerusalem echo the pant and screech of the locomotive, which now connects the Holy City with Jaffa on the Mediterranean; and probably it will not be long before a trolley line will connect the site of Solomon's capital with a line of steamboats on the Dead sea, which has so long remained a forsaken solitude in the midst of a desert. At the other end of Asia, Japan, since opening her arms to the progressive West, is thriving with manufacturing and other developing industries, and has recently stood forth as the little giant of the Orient. In 1894, disputing with China the protectorate of Corea, she sent her well-drilled and well-equipped troops to sustain her claims, soon occupied all Corea, Port Arthur, part of Manchuria and Wei-hai-Wei, and by the treaty of Shimonosaki (in April, 1895), induced China to cede Formosa, the Pescadores, and the peninsula of Liao-tung, to open new ports, to permit the erection of Japanese manufacturing establishments in the empire, and to agree to pay a war indemnity of seven hundred and fifty millions. She surprised the world by the rapidity of her success, but she was soon persuaded, by the concerted " friendly " protest of Russia, France and Germany, to modify the treaty and relinquish Liao-tung and Wei-hai-Wei.

China, awakening from the lethargy of ages, observes that the face of the world has changed, and is preparing for regeneration from a long rule of ultra conservatism.[1] She will soon be threaded with railways, and brought into closer touch with Western civilization. She has granted to Great Britain the privilege of building railroads in the valley of the Yang-tse, and has made concessions to other nations for roads in other parts of the empire. In 1896, she granted to the Eastern Chinese Railroad Company the right to build a line through Chinese Manchuria (to connect as a branch of the Trans-Siberian Railway), to develop coal and other mines in the adjoining territory, and to engage in other industrial and commercial enterprises. In 1898, she granted to Russia the privilege of building a railway from Vladivostock to Port Arthur. More recently she agreed to permit the construction of a line from Mukden in Manchuria to Peking, and three lines from Peking to the provinces of Shansi, Ho-nan and Hupeh. Still other lines are in contemplation to connect southern China with Peking, with French Indo-China, and with Burma of British India.

The " Eastern Question " has spread from Constantinople and the eastern shores of the Mediterranean to Persia, Afghanistan, and the Far East. It has expanded or resolved itself into many problems, of which the Chinese has recently become the most prominent. Of the nominally independent countries of Asia, *i. e.*, Turkey, Arabia, Oman, Persia, Afghanistan, Nepal, Bhutan, Siam, China, Corea and Japan —only Japan is thoroughly independent in fact. European powers have zones of influence in all of the others. Turkey, in need of a better government, has been the object of the

---

[1] A. R. Calquhoun: China in Transformation. Curzon: Problems of the Far East. Lord Charles Beresford: The Break-up of China.

deliberations of an international congress. Central Arabia is inhabited by tribes who owe allegiance to no single ruler. Oman is practically an English protectorate. Persia is dominated by Russia in the north and by England in the south. Afghanistan, under the uncertain rule of an Afghan chief, receives a subsidy from British India, and permits a Russian flotilla on her branches of the Oxus. Some say that occupation or protection by some stronger power is apparently the only relief for the chaotic conditions which exist from the Bosporus to the Hindu Kush. China, though not in the same political condition as Turkey and Persia, sometimes appears to be preparing herself for a coroner's inquest or vivisection. Her internal condition, together with her relation to opposing powers with conflicting interests, presents a serious case to the political doctors, who find it difficult to agree upon a remedy to effect a permanent cure.

The Anglo-Saxon and the Slav have met on the Plains of Pamir, the roof of the world, at the western gate of China. Only a strip of Afghan territory, twelve miles wide, lies between them, and it is under British influence. Afghanistan is only a temporary " buffer " between them, though it may be of little value to either except as a basis for military operations. With half-completed military roads, they keep their armies like bridled steeds, ready to prance toward each other in war-harness. The Anglo-Saxon nation, incessantly toiling, cultivating swamps and clearing jungles, driving back famine and pestilence, and opening the tropics to the world, has extended her dominion upward from the south of India, secured a supreme influence in Southern Asia from the Red Sea coast and the Persian Gulf on the west to Siam and toward Singapore on the east. She has peacefully expanded over Beluchistan, and extended her control northward from Calcutta to the Himalayas and eastward to Siam. Still further east she possesses Borneo and South Sea groups of islands. In China, she is already established at Hong Kong, has a shadowy sphere of predominating influence in the Yang-tse valley, and is planning to secure a concession for a railway from Burma to Yunnan.

The Slav, by a long record of toil and privation and self-directed effort, has colonized central Asia and continued eastward with half-accidental, half-unconscious progress across the continent. Vast Russia, virile, apparently invincible, and increasingly predominant, spanning Europe and Asia, embracing one-half the combined area of the two continents (and nearly two and one-half times as large as the United States), is steadily expanding to the south and east along a wavering frontier of 10,000 miles. She is strengthening her hand in the Bosporus, Syria and Palestine and in Persia, which offers a practicable trade outlet to the Indian ocean, and an advantage in case of conflict with England. If England and France would permit, she would absorb Turkey, whose capital she has threatened for 800 years. She has become predominant in the north of Persia, whose territory she has been acquiring for 100 years. She has consolidated her position in Turkestan, elbowed China out of Pamir on the west. The more England has hindered her in the south, the better has she established herself in the east, especially since the Crimean war. In her search for a " scientific boundary," she has always advocated " rectification of the frontier " as a remedy for grievances, and is now in possession of the greater part of the land which China has been losing since 1858. Indenting Chinese territory from Pamir to Manchuria, she has been making rapid strides to occupy the position once held by Genghiz Khan.[2]

Russia is now at the beginning of a new era in her history. Since 1893, she has been consolidating the work of the early venturesome explorers across the wilds of Siberia by the construction of a trans-Siberian railway with numerous stations and branches. By means of this road she is securing a more rapid colonization of Siberia—whose fertile,

---

[2] Alexia Krausse: Russia in Asia (1558-1899).

productive lands no longer remain locked in silence and solitude—and is expecting to work a revolution in the commerce and travel of the world. She is bringing the Far East to the doors of Europe, and preparing to become an oceanic power. After a struggle of 200 years to reach the open sea, and a port free from ice at all seasons of the year, she now floats her flag over Port Arthur, southeast of Peking, and is attaining the freedom of the seas.

Russia now threatens to secure an advantage in the trade of China by a process of gradual absorption. She has rapidly become a manufacturing nation, and, like Great Britain and the United States and other powers, is seeking new markets. She claims a sphere of influence north and east of Peking, and has an eye toward the great central valley where British influence is still predominant. Knowing that it will be difficult for her, under equal terms, to compete with British, American, German and French trade, she may undertake to secure exclusive privileges for her traders and for the exercise of her influence, and perhaps obtain complete control of portions of China under an exclusive colonial system. In case she should become involved in a conflict with Great Britain, who has so long been her competitor and antagonist in the direction of Asia, she would probably have the assistance of France, who, driven from India by the British, and profiting by fortunate circumstances, has established a new French empire in the Indo-Chinese peninsula (including Cambodia, Anam, Cochin China and Tonkin), and has a sphere of commercial activity in the south of China. Russia and France, should they form an alliance for the partition of China, would probably be resisted by the common action of Great Britain and Japan, and also by Germany in case such action should seem to be subordinate to her European and general interests.

The United States, though beginning to play a great part in the Pacific, and having trade interests in the Orient which may increase rapidly, desires to remain free to act independently, or in cooperation, as circumstances may indicate to be the wisest policy. She feels, however, that her position among the nations,with a large Pacific coast and a constantly expanding direct trade with the Far East, gives her " an equitable claim to consideration and friendly treatment." She finds an open door along the shores of southern Asia, where Great Britain has control, and perhaps would participate in active cooperation to prevent any power from securing exclusive commercial advantages in China. She " has not been an indifferent spectator of the extraordinary events transpiring in China," by which portions of the maritime provinces are passing under the control of various European powers; but the necessity of her becoming an " actor in the scene " has been obviated by the prospect that the new occupants will not prejudice American commerce by exclusive treatment.[3]

The United States, through her prestige as a territorially disinterested power, and her ability to speak in the language of unselfish, powerful diplomacy, has an opportunity to become an arbiter in a peaceful and definite settlement of the problems of the Far East, securing fair dealing and equal opportunity, and preserving the honor and interests of all. Facing Asia as well as Europe, she is well situated for the protection of American interests and the support of the independence and integrity of China with an open door to commerce—a policy which the American Government has advocated for over thirty years.[4] With her western coast ports, the Hawaiian and Philippine islands, and steamers on the Pacific, if she prepare to urge an open-door, non-partition policy in China, she can secure her share of the developing trade of the Orient.

The importance of securing ports or establishments in the vicinity of the coasts of Asia, for the benefit of American commerce, was suggested in the early part of the century. It was urged in 1832 by President Jackson, who sent Ed-

---

[3] President McKinley's message, Dec. 5, 1898.
[4] Instr. Germany, Fish to Bancroft, Aug. 31, 1869.

mund Roberts to negotiate treaties with Borneo, Siam, Cochin China and Japan. The increase of American interest in the Orient, by the conditions following American expansion to California, soon resulted in a determination to secure better facilities for intercourse with the Pacific and the Eastern countries. "The future history of the world must be achieved in the East," said W. H. Trescot, who urged (1849) the policy of an Anglo-American alliance as a means to prevent Russian designs in China and to "control the history of the world." Senator Seward, advocating surveys in the seas of the Far East, in 1852, said: "Who does not see, then, that every year hereafter, European commerce, European politics, European thought, and European activity, although actually gaining force, and European connections, although actually becoming more intimate, will, nevertheless, relatively sink in importance; while the Pacific ocean, its shores, its islands and the vast region beyond will become the chief theatre of events in the world's great Hereafter. . . . Who does not see that this movement must . . . develop the American opinion and influence, which shall remould constitutional laws and customs in the land which is first greeted by the rising sun . . . I cannot reject the hope that peace is now to have her sway. . . . Commerce is the great agent of this movement. Whatever nation shall put that commerce into full employment, and shall conduct it steadily with adequate expansion, shall become necessarily the greatest of existing States." Commodore Perry, on his route to secure ports in Japan, proposed the occupation of the Loo Choo Islands as a preliminary measure, and also contemplated the extension of American jurisdiction over the Bonin group. Later he suggested the occupation and colonization of Formosa. In 1856 and 1857, Mr. Parker, the American commissioner in China, suggested to Secretary Marcy the policy of taking Formosa from China as an indemnity [supra, p. 98]. Marcy had just been making an effort to acquire Hawaii, as an outlying territorial possession with no promise of statehood, but he was opposed to the seizure of Formosa. The peaceful negotiation of treaties with Japan and China, after 1857, reduced the immediate importance of securing ports on the smaller islands as proposed by Perry. The annexation of Hawaii, however, continued to be regarded as a measure concomitant with the increase of American influence in the Pacific. In reply to those who opposed its annexation because of its distant insular position, Senator Dolph, in 1893, said: "We must abandon the doctrine that our national boundaries and jurisdiction should be confined to the shores of the continent. We cannot afford, like a snail, to draw our heads within our shells." At the beginning of 1898, Senator Lodge said that since we had made the citadel secure, we must not now neglect the outposts.

By the retention of the Philippines, the United States has entered upon a new era. Refusing to choose a policy of isolation, she has become a world power, and a leading factor in international politics. She no longer stands aloof from the Pacific, " the historic sea of the future," [5] as she did in her weak beginnings when the vast unexplored territories on our west belonged to foreign powers.

Her evolution to the " Great Pacific Power " appears to be but the logic of history. Richard Olney, ex-Secretary of State, recently referring to our future relations with the European powers struggling for commercial and political supremacy in the East, said the abandonment of our " international isolation " policy, which was only suited to the period of our infancy, was inevitable, and would result in

---

[5] " The nations have their toes toward the Pacific." They have left very few of its islands unappropriated. Since the race for island-grabbing in the South Seas, in 1884-86, there is no longer an opportunity to occupy fabled regions unexplored in the Polynesian world. The nations have been taking time by the forelock and preparing to secure positions which are likely to prove advantageous in connection with the swiftly changing conditions in the Orient.

aiding our commercial interests and the widening of our mental and moral vision as a nation.

The constitutional question involved in the acquisition and government of the Philippines has recently been the subject of much discussion. It will soon be a subject of decision by the Supreme Court. The American Government is acting upon the belief that the islands can be governed by Congress as territorial possessions of the United States, and in beginning the inauguration of a responsible government has very liberal views.[6] It proposes a political system devised for the interest of all concerned and administered by the inhabitants as far as they show a capacity for self-government; but, if necessary to preserve order, the islands may be ruled by the American Government with a hand as strong as that of Jefferson, who applied his " despotic " non-representative system to Louisiana against the protests of the inhabitants, who requested him to send the Declaration of Independence and the Constitution to the shores of the Mississippi.

America faces responsibility and opportunity with the same spirit of confidence which animated the Fathers. With her face set toward the morning, she seeks duty with the courage of the optimist and the ameliorator. She does not let her aspirations sink before the predictions of the prophets

---

[6] In his message of Dec., 1899, President McKinley said:

" The hour of victory will be the hour of clemency and reconstruction.

" No effort will be spared to build up the waste places desolated by the war and by long years of misgovernment. We shall not wait for the end of the strife to begin the beneficent work. We shall continue, as we have begun, to open the schools and the churches, to set the courts in operation, to foster industry and trade and agriculture, and in every way in our power to make these people, whom Providence has brought within our jurisdiction, feel that it is their liberty and not our power, their welfare and not our gain, we are seeking to enhance.

" Our flag has never waved over any community but in blessing. I feel the Filipinos will soon recognize the fact that it has not lost its gift of benediction in its world-wide journey to their shores."

of disaster.   She has not become discouraged by the gloomy views of "trembling ones shrieking at the self-conjured ghost of imperialism, as if empire could grow on freedom's soil."   She sees no reason to condemn the present or to despair of the future.   She observes that the republic has survived the predictions of disaster made by those who opposed the policy of Jefferson, Madison, Monroe and their successors.   She asserts that the Ship of State under sunny skies still has her anchors, and is abundantly able to meet new conditions in world movements.

The future belongs to the future.   Its conditions will influence the shaping of policy for the solution of problems as they arise.   But America has no element of exploitation or imperialism lurking in her purposes.   With high and just motives, she reaches the hand of helpfulness across the seas which she wishes to transform into paths for ships. She will continue to embark, venture, explore and investigate, as she has in the past.   She will carefully survey and feel her way, and construct charts for those who follow. With the strenuous spirit of the pioneer, she advances beyond the frontier.   When she reaches streams unspanned, she will build bridges; and when she comes to bridges, she will cross them.

The descendants and beneficiaries of those who, three centuries ago, animated with the desire to found an imperial democracy, faced the cold, inhospitable coasts of a wild, uncivilized continent and began our traditional policy of expansion, may confidently face the problems of foreign policy and territorial government which now confront them.

APPENDIX A.

Instructions to Humphrey Marshall as Commissioner to China in 1852–53.[1]

DEPARTMENT OF STATE,
WASHINGTON, 11TH AUGUST, 1852.

No. 1.   HUMPHREY MARSHALL, ESQ.,
ETC., ETC.

Sir:—The Department [has] already communicated to you your Commission as Commissioner of the United States of America to China.

Your compensation as fixed by law is at the rate of Six Thousand Dollars ($6000) per annum.   . . .

To become properly conversant with the business of the Legation, you will have recourse to the correspondence between this Department and your predecessors in the Mission, recorded in its archives.   Special instructions on important subjects between the two Governments will be sent to you from time to time as occasion may require.

During your residence in China, you may sometimes be applied to to interpose in behalf of American citizens for the purpose of obtaining satisfaction of claims which they may have upon the Chinese Government, or the redress of grievances which they may experience in the course of their dealings and transactions.   In cases of this nature, where the intervention of this Government shall be proper according to the public law, you will afford such official aid as may appear to you appropriate to the occasion whether you have special instructions from this Department or not.   . . .

I am Sir, respectfully,

Your obedient servant,

DAN^L WEBSTER.

[1 China Instr., pp. 76–79.]   . . .

---

[1] Before the appointment of Marshall, the position had been offered to three persons within one year. The nomination of A. R. Nelson was confirmed by the Senate in March, 1851. Joseph Blunt accepted the place on October 20, 1851. On February 24, 1852, the President offered the place to Alfred Conkling, of New York, who declined. Marshall's commission was sent to him by the Department of State on August 6, 1852. See p. 90, *supra.*

DEPARTMENT OF STATE,
WASHINGTON, 20TH SEPT., 1852.

No. 2.   HUMPHREY MARSHALL, ESQ.,
ETC., ETC.

Sir :—You are aware that some of our citizens now or formerly resident in China, have, for a long time past had claims against the Chinese Government. The cases are that of the Rev. Mr. Roberts for losses sustained by a mob at Canton, and that of Messrs. Louis Manigault and Edward Cunningham, for assault and robbery in the neighborhood of the same city. The Department is not in possession of such proof as would warrant it in expressing an opinion in regard to these claims. As you will be on the spot, however, where all the evidence that can be adduced in support of them will be accessible to you, you will be enabled to determine whether they are of such a character as would warrant the official interposition of this Government. It is possible that the Chinese Government might require proof of your authority to negotiate upon the subject. To provide for this contingency, it has been judged expedient to give you the accompanying full power. This will enable you to adjust not only the cause above mentioned, but any others which may occur during your mission.

I am Sir, respectfully,

Your obedient servant,

C. M. CONRAD,
Acting Secretary.

[1 China Instr., pp. 79–80.]

DEPARTMENT OF STATE,
WASHINGTON, 7TH JUNE, 1853.

No. 8.   HUMPHREY MARSHALL, ESQ.,
ETC., ETC.

Sir :—Your despatches to No. 10, inclusive, have been duly received at this Department.

The Government of the United States has recently received additional information of the successful progress of the Revolutionary movements in China. It is also apprised of the intention of the Government of Great Britain to avail itself of the present condition of things in that country to obtain "increased facilities of intercourse" with it, not exclusively for its own subjects but for all nations and it has suggested to this Government to send such instructions to our Commissioner there as will "empower him to take such course in conjunction with Her Majesty's Plenipotentiary as will be calculated to turn to the best account the opportunity offered by the present crisis to open the Chinese Empire generally to the commercial enterprise of all of the civilized nations of the world."

The end proposed commends itself to the approval of the President and he directs you to do what you can within your proper sphere of action, towards its accomplishment. Our treaty stipulations with China must be respected and our settled policy of non-interference in the contests which arise between the people and their rulers must be observed. Without a departure from these rules of conduct you may be able to do much in such a crisis as does or may exist in China to cause an abandonment of the unwise restrictions imposed by China upon foreign intercourse. Without knowing what course the British authorities may deem it expedient to take in furtherance of the object in view, the President does not enjoin upon you cooperation, but only cordial relations and free conference with them.

As it is impossible to anticipate here what will be the condition of things there, no specific instructions in regard to your official conduct can be given. Your own judgment must be your guide as to the best means to accomplish the desired object.

In the agitated state of the country the property of our citizens therein and their rights will probably be in unusual danger. You will be vigilant and active in affording them all the protection within your power. The naval force of the United States in that vicinity will be devoted to this important object.

The Department requests you to keep it fully advised of the progress of events in China, of the effects of the Revolutionary proceedings there upon our interests and of the prospects presented for a more free and extended commerce with that country.

I am Sir, respectfully,
Your obedient servant,
W. L. MARCY.

[1 China Instr., pp. 84–86.]

APPENDIX B.

GOVERNMENT OF HAWAII AS A TERRITORY OF THE UNITED STATES.[1]

Congress in providing for the government of Hawaii as an American Territory has been very liberal. In the original bill as presented by the commissioners who visited the island, strong argument was presented in favor of a property qualification for voters. It was feared that natives, with suffrage unrestricted, would secure the control of the legislature, and might even be able to override the veto of the governor. It was said that if the natives should combine, it was reasonable to suppose that no white person could be elected to a legislative seat.

After the overthrow of the monarchy a property qualification had been imposed upon the electors of senators. A conservative class was thus provided, and held the other house in check. The system was recommended for continuation.

The Congressional committee to which the Hawaiian bill was referred did not retain the property-qualification feature. It acted upon the principle that "the right of free expression at the polls is in the nature of a safety valve," and that citizens of Hawaii should have the right to participate in their government, irrespective of tax-paying ability. Hawaii had already shown herself capable of maintaining a stable government. She had a system of laws based upon American laws. She was familiar with Anglo-Saxon institutions and language. She had voluntarily placed herself under the sovereignty of the United States. Americans, although in a small minority, practically dominated the governmental, financial and commercial affairs of the islands.[2]

Congress had never yet required a property qualification in any of the territories, (though in some cases there had been reason to suspect the danger of riotous and ignorant legislation), and it was not considered necessary to make a local exception in the case of Hawaii.

---

[1] See p. 134 *supra*

[2] The Hawaiian Islands are now occupied by the following races and nationalities:

Hawaiians and mixed blood	39,000
Japanese	25,000
Chinese	21,000
Portuguese	15,000
Americans	4,000
British	2,250
Germans and other Europeans	2,000
Polynesians and miscellaneous	1,250
Total	109,500

About 700 Chinese have been naturalized into the Hawaiian republic, and many Chinese and Japanese are there under government permits and labor contracts, under which they are bound to work for a term of years and to return to their own countries at the end of their term of service.

The Chinese and Japanese possess no political power.

The Portuguese are largely immigrants or descendants from immigrants from the islands and colonies of Portugal in the Atlantic and are not closely allied in sentiment to their native country.

The public school system makes the study of the English language compulsory. There are 132 public and 60 private schools, and education is compulsory and free as to all public schools. American text-books are used in the schools. The language of business in English and the decisions of American courts prevail as precedents.

GOVERNMENT
OF THE
TERRITORY OF HAWAII
(April 30, 1900)

1. LEGISLATURE

CONSISTS OF TWO HOUSES.
(Section 12)

Provisions common to both houses: General elections, first Tuesday after first Monday in November, 1900, and biennially thereafter (14). Each house judge of election, returns, and qualifications of own members (15). Can not hold other office (16–17). Oath of office (19). Each determines its own rules. One-fifth can demand ayes and noes. Majority constitutes quorum for business, except on final passage; then majority of all members required (22). Less than quorum may adjourn and compel attendance (23). Each house punishes members (25). Members exempt from liability elsewhere for words (28). Arrest (29). Salary, $400 each session and 10 cents a mile each way; $200 extra session.

First session, third Wednesday, February, 1901, and biennially thereafter (41). Special session may be convened (43). Sessions 60 days long, except that governor may extend 30 days (43). All proceedings in English language (44). Bills must pass three readings on separate days (46), and final passage must be on majority vote of all members by ayes and noes. Governor may veto appropriation bills in whole or in part (49). Bills may be passed over veto by two-thirds vote (50).

Scope of power.

"Shall extend to all rightful subjects of legislation not inconsistent with the Constitution and laws of the United States locally applicable."

May create counties and town and city municipalities, and provide for the government thereof.

Senate — Composed of 15 members: 4 years; elected from 4 districts, alternating 7 and 8 biennially (30, 32). Vacancies filled by election (31). Must be male citizens of United States, 30 years old, resided in Hawaii 3 years, qualified to vote for senators (34).

Voting for senators. — Each voter may cast one vote for each senator from district (61), and required number of candidates receiving highest number of votes shall be senators in district (61). Voters must have qualifications of voters for representatives, i. e., male citizen of the United States, residence 1 year in Hawaii, 3 months in district, 21 years old (60–62); must register, and be able to speak, read, and write English or Hawaiian (60).

House — Composed of 30 members, elected from 6 districts every second year (35). Term until next general election (36, 38). Vacancies filled at general or special elections (37); must be male citizens of United States, 25 years old, resided in Hawaii 3 years, and qualified to vote for representatives (40).

Voting for representatives. — Each voter may cast a vote for as many representatives as are to be elected from district (59), and required number of candidates receiving highest number of votes are elected (59). Voters, male citizens of the United States, 21 years old, have resided in Hawaii 1 year, and in district 3 months; have registered, and able to speak, read, and write English or Hawaiian.

Special limitations

1. The legislature shall not grant any special or exclusive privilege, immunity or franchise without the approval of Congress.
2. It shall not grant private charters, but may pass general acts governing corporations.
3. It shall not grant divorces.
4. It shall not grant money for sectarian or private schools.
5. The Government, or any political or municipal corporation or subdivision of the Territory, shall not make any subscription to the capital stock of any corporation, nor lend its credit therefor.
6. The legislature shall not authorize any debt to be contracted except to pay interest upon existing indebtedness, to suppress insurrection, or to provide for the common defense—and except loans for the erection of penal, charitable and educational institutions, and for public works.

2. THE EXECUTIVE.

Governor (Sec. 66).

Appointed by President for 4 years and until successor is appointed and qualified. Shall be 35 years old and citizen of Hawaii. Salary, $5,000 (92); $500 incidentals, traveling, and $2,000 for private secretary.

Powers and duties (66, 67).

Shall be commander-in-chief of militia; may grant pardons or reprieves for offenses against Territory and against United States, pending decision by President. When necessary may call upon military or naval forces of the United States in Hawaii, or summon posse comitatus, or call out militia; may suspend writ of habeas corpus or place Territory under martial law; has veto power; power of removal when not otherwise provided (80).

Appointive power (80).

1. Judges circuit courts.
2. Attorney-general.
3. Treasurer.
4. Commissioner of public lands.
5. Commissioner of agriculture.
6. Superintendent of public works.
7. Superintendent of public instruction.
8. Auditor.
9. Deputy auditor.
10. Surveyor.
11. High sheriff.
12. Members board of health.
13. Commissioners of public instruction.
14. Boards of registration and inspectors of elections.
15. All other public boards.

Secretary (66).

Appointed by President for 4 years and until successor is appointed and qualified. Salary, $3,000 (92).

Duties and powers.

Shall record and preserve all the acts and proceedings of the legislature and the governor, promulgate proclamations, and transmit to the President of the United States copies of the laws, journals, and executive proceedings.

Shall act as governor in case of vacancy by death, removal, resignation, disability or absence of the governor.

Other executive officers Appointed by the Governor for 4 years (80).

Attorney-general (71).
Treasurer (72).
Commissioner of public lands (73).
Commissioner of agriculture and forestry (74).
Superintendent of public works (75).
Superintendent of public instruction (76).
Auditor and deputy auditor (77).
Surveyor (78).
High sheriff (79).

3. THE JUDICIARY.

Hawaiian laws relative to, are continued in force, except as modified by this Act; subject to modification by Congress or legislature (83).

No person can sit as judge or juror who is related by affinity or consanguinity to parties within third degree or who shall be interested pecuniarily, personally, or through relatives who are parties (84).

Hawaiian Courts (81).

1. Supreme court: One chief justice (salary $5,500), and two associates (salaries $5,000), appointed by the President of the United States by and with advice and consent of the Senate (82), and hold 4 years (80).
2. Circuit courts: The judges are appointed by the governor, and hold for 4 years (80).
3. Such inferior courts as the legislature shall from time to time establish (81).

Federal District Court (86).

President of the United States, by and with advice and consent of the Senate, shall appoint district judge (86). Shall have jurisdiction of cases commonly cognizable by both circuit and district courts (86).

Writs of error and appeals shall be had and allowed to the circuit court of appeals in the ninth judicial circuit of the United States.

District attorney, salary $3,000, and marshal, salary $2,500 (92), appointed by the President, by and with the advice and consent of the Senate (86).

The district judge shall appoint a clerk (salary $3,000) and a reporter (salary $1200).

The total indebtedness that may be incurred in any one year by the Territory, or any such subdivision thereof, is limited to 1 per cent of the taxable property of the Territory or any such subdivision as shown by the last general assessment; and the total indebtedness of the Territory at any one time shall not exceed 7 per cent of assessed valuation; nor shall the total indebtedness of any such subdivision of the Territory at any one time exceed 3 per cent of any such assessed valuation. However, the Governwent is not prevented from refunding existing indebtedness at any time.

No loans are to be made upon the public domain, and no bonds or other instruments of indebtedness are to be issued unless redeemable in five years, payable in fifteen years, and approved by the President of the United States.

SPECIAL TOPICS.

1. Delegate to Congress.

There shall be a delegate to the United States House of Representatives (to be elected by voters qualified to vote for members of the house of representatives of Hawaii), who shall possess qualifications of members of the senate of Hawaii; time, place, and manner of holding elections fixed by law (85).

2. Internal-revenue district.

The) Territory shall constitute an internal-revenue district (87).

3. Customs district.

The Territory shall constitute a customs district with ports of entry and delivery at Honolulu, Hilo Makukona, and Kahului (88).

4. Wharves.

Wharves and landings shall remain under control of Hawaii, and revenues derived therefrom shall belong to Hawaii, provided same are applied to their maintenance and repair (89).

5. Quarantine.

The quarantine regulations relating to the importation of diseases from other countries shall be under the control of the Government of the United States; but the health laws of the government of Hawaii relating to harbors and internal control shall remain in the jurisdiction of the government of Hawaii, subject to the quarantine laws and regulations of the United States (97).

6. Naturalization.	Previous residence in Hawaii shall be deemed equivalent to residence in the United States. The American regulation requiring a previous declaration of intention to become a citizen of the United States, etc., shall "not apply to persons who have resided in the islands at least five years prior to the taking effect of this Act" (100).
7. Chinese certificates of residence.	Chinese in Hawaiian Islands given one year to obtain certificates of residence as provided by the Act of Congress approved May 5, 1892, and amended November 3, 1893; but "no Chinese laborer, whether he shall hold such certificate, or not, shall be allowed to enter any State, Territory, or District of the United States from the Hawaiian Islands" (101).

The provision (Sec. 6) extending the Constitution and laws of the United States placed the Chinese-exclusion law and the alien contract-labor law immediately in force in the Territory of Hawaii.

The joint resolution of annexation provided that there should be no further immigration of Chinese into Hawaii except as allowed by the laws of the United States, and that no Chinese, by virtue of anything contained in the joint resolution of annexation, should come to the United States from Hawaii.

8. Hawaiian public lands.

The public-land system of the United States has not been extended to Hawaii. In some respects it is entirely inapplicable. It would be difficult to establish an arbitrary rectangular system upon a peculiar system long in practice.

The public-land system of Hawaii evolved from local conditions. The lands are already occupied, and, from the very nature of the soil and character of the inhabitants, are cut up into holdings of all sizes, the shape being generally that of an irregular triangle, with its base on the coast line and its apex toward the centre of the island.

There has already been established there a system of survey adapted to the natural formation and contour of the islands. For illustration, all the islands rise from the sea level, in some parts abruptly and in some parts gradually, to a central elevation, and for purposes of cultivation the land is naturally divided into lowland, fitted for the growth of taro and rice; next above this is sugar land, next coffee land, and then comes grazing and timber land.

Up to 1846 all the lands of the Hawaiian Islands belonged in legal contemplation to the king. The chiefs and the people, under a feudal system closely resembling the old English feudal system, held their respective parcels by rendering service or payment of rent. In 1846 King Kamehameha III. granted: (1) To his chiefs and people certain portions; (2) for government purposes certain portions, (3) and reserved the remainder.

By an act, June 7, 1848, the legislature accepted the king's grant and confirmed to the king, his heirs and successors, certain described lands which were thenceforth known as crown lands. Under an act organizing executive departments, a land commission was provided whose duty it was to receive and pass upon the claims of occupants and lands to their respective holdings in that portion of the land set apart for the chiefs and people. This commission heard the testimony of claimants, caused surveys to be made, and issued to the occupants entitled thereto certificates called "Land commission awards." These awards established the right of the grantee to the possession of the land and entitled him upon payment of one-fourth of the value of the bare land to receive a royal patent. These awards and patents issued pursuant thereto are the source of all title to all lands not public lands or crown lands.

By an act of July 9, 1850, one-twentieth of all public lands are set apart for the support of schools. These lands are patented to a board of education, which was empowered to sell and lease. Part of these lands is used for sites for school buildings, part is leased, and part has been sold.

In 1884 a homestead law on a small scale was provided but was little used, only 256 patents having been issued in sixteen years.

In 1894, the legislature passed " the land act of 1895." By this act the crown lands were treated as having vested in the republic and were placed under the control of a board of commissioners, composed of the secretary of the interior and two persons appointed by the governor. They are now embraced as public lands, and are under the control of a commissioner of public lands. They are subject to alienation and other uses as may be provided by law (99).

The islands are divided into six land districts, with a subagent of public lands and ranges for each.

The public domain is divided into agricultural, pastoral, pastoral-agricultural, forest and waste lands.

The commissioners are authorized to dispose of these lands in the following manner:

1. At public auction for cash in parcels not exceeding 1,000 acres.

2. At public auction, part credit, in parcels not exceeding 600 acres.

3. Without auction sale, in exchange for private lands or by way of compromise.

4. By lease at public auction for not more than twenty-one years.

5. Homestead leases.

6. Right-of-purchase leases.

7. Cash freeholds.

Under the act of Congress approved April 30, 1900, the commissioner of public lands takes the place of the board of commissioners. The laws relating to public lands, the settlement of boundaries, and the issuance of patents on land-commission awards continue in force until Congress shall provide otherwise. But " no lease of agricultural land shall be granted, sold, or renewed by the government of the Territory of Hawaii for a longer period than five years until Congress shall otherwise direct." All funds arising from this disposal of such lands shall be appropriated by the Hawaiian government and applied for the benefit of the inhabitants (73).

SUBJECT INDEX